SCOTLAND LIVES

SCOTLAND LIVES

BILLY WOLFE

*This book is dedicated to the men, women and children
who have given me the inspiration and encouragement
to continue the struggle for an independent Scotland*

23 Livingstone Place, Edinburgh EH9 1PD
Scotland
1973

SBN 903065 09 6

Cover illustration and design
by G. Gordon Wright

Printed in Scotland by
Macdonald Printers (Edinburgh) Limited
Edgefield Road, Loanhead, Midlothian

CONTENTS

CHAPTER 1

THE YEARS BEFORE

ON MY THIRTY-EIGHTH birthday in February 1962, my horizons were those of the average citizen who takes part in the life of his community. To me, active politicians were a race apart—people whom one only met occasionally. Little did I know that within a few days, I would be taking a first step to join that race apart. Life for my wife and myself has never been the same since.

When I was demobilised in 1947 I became active in the Saltire Society and became aware of the continuing erosion of our Scottish identity in the whole fabric of community life. I saw a handful of people striving in this voluntary society, trying to persuade governments and their departments, local authorities, universities, schools, colleges and the general public at large, that Scotland had an identity and cultural heritage which it was the responsibility of the present generation to preserve, to learn from and develop in the interests of humanity.

By 1959, I had become sceptical about the work of the Saltire Society. The labours of the few in this particular vineyard were not influencing the forces which shaped the lives of the people of Scotland. Unemployment caused high emigration, mostly of educated and skilled people who were taking part of Scotland's future with them, usually for ever. There were terrible slums in Scotland and there was a widespread and weakening lack of confidence in the future of the country.

Previously I had known almost nothing about politics, but my years with the Saltire Society had taught me something of the essence of Scotland. Active participation in church work had taught me something of the needs of people. Devotion to the ideals of brotherhood within the Scout movement taught me the aspirations and difficulties of youth, and sharing family life with a wife and children taught me more about love than I had ever expected.

All these aspects of my life, together with the experience of five years in the British Army (1942 - 47, on active service in Western Europe and the Far East), my training as a Chartered Accountant and subsequent work in a manufacturing business owned by other members of my family, formed a pattern of

7

living which fell short of satisfaction. The irritation which spoiled the picture was the sense of fighting a losing battle in which I was constantly defending the right to be a Scotsman. It irked me that it should be necessary for anyone to fight to be himself.

I could recall in my childhood, as a Scout, being irritated by the imposition of an English outlook in what was supposed to be an international brotherhood. I could look back on Army service in which I had made many friendships with Englishmen, yet in which I was constantly exposed to the English middle-class assertion that the anglicised (they called it "the civilised") Scot was the best kind of person in the world (a world in which only English was spoken). I could remember enthusiastically collecting signatures on the Covenant for the re-establishment of a Scottish Parliament; and could not forget the disappointment at the achievement of almost nothing in the way of progress by those two million signatures.

I wrote to the five political parties and asked for their policies for Scotland and in turn five manifestos were read and studied. I had been neither left nor right, consciously, in my views and beliefs before, but as far as I was concerned, the Scottish National Party's manifesto was the only one which offered the realisation of all my aspirations and dreams for the re-birth of Scotland.

I joined the Scottish National Party, convinced that "There is a nation of Scots, therefore to survive, that nation must behave like other nations and accept the responsibilities of nationhood." I realised that self-government was an essential part of the self-expression of the Scots, if they were not to disappear in an ever-increasing suffocation of anglicisation. Scotland was becoming more and more a province of England, and I realised that only the SNP offered a positive, honest and uncompromising approach to the re-establishment of a sovereign Scottish Parliament.

My home has been in Torphichen since marriage; I was born in Bathgate, three miles away, but my wife Maimie and I set up home in this ancient village in 1953. It is situated in what many regard as the heartland of Scotland; people have lived in and around Torphichen for 5000 years, and have left memorials of different kinds as evidence of their presence. History records little of Torphichen in writing, but stones and legends stretch our roots back through the centuries.

Torphichen was peopled by miners, weavers and farmers in the nineteenth and eighteenth centuries, by Covenanters in the seventeenth, by the Order of St John from the sixteenth down to the twelfth, and by early Christian endeavour right back to the land of Manau Gododdin in Arthurian times; before then, the transient Roman visitors, and so back to the men who built a monument at Cairnpapple, 5000 or so years ago—among the earliest men to settle in what we now call Scotland. Prominent on the stage are William Wallace, whose only surviving signature as Guardian of Scotland was signed in Torphichen Preceptory; Edward the Hammer who spent at least one night in the same place; Sir James Sandilands, the last Preceptor of the Order of St John, in whose ancestral home at Calder, a few miles away, Reformers first celebrated Communion according to their revised rites; Henry Bell, the builder of "The Comet," the world's first practical steamship, who was born and grew up here; and many other worthy men and women, ministers and common folk, knights, soldiers and bairns.

Torphichen Preceptory had the right of sanctuary in medieval days, and to mark the boundaries of the privilege, four massive stones were set and marked a mile or so from the central "Refuge Stone," which was probably an altar stone in pre-Christian days, and which still stands in the kirkyard. Torphichen is no longer a sanctuary for those pursued in rough justice, but it is still a living Scottish community. No fugitives come here now, but if there is to be a future of social justice as well as legal justice for the people, not only of Torphichen but of all Scotland and all mankind, there has to be an outgoing of the spirit, a dedication to better things, and that is what this book is about.

CHAPTER 2

MY FIRST CAMPAIGN,
WEST LOTHIAN, 1962

THE ELECTRICIANS had gone. My wife told me they had been, but I hadn't noticed, lying there losing twenty-four hours or more at the height of the fever. I was past the peak and feeling I could read, so I read *Sunset Song* for the first time. I had heard it on the radio about twelve years before, and I had been deeply moved. I bought the book at the time, but the memory of those voices telling the story of a Scotland that was passing had kept me from reading it.

Now, a few days after my birthday in 1962, as I recovered from some special kind of 'flu, I read the trilogy. This time, I was moved to indignation and frustration, not because of the loss of old and hard ways of life, but because I realised anew that the essence of Scotland was being so diluted and near destroyed without the people, the real folk of Scotland, being able to do anything about it. It was a kindly English imperialism that was destroying them, and their own vulnerability was making it so easy.

Two or three days later, Robert Kerr called to see me. He had called with a *Scots Independent* practically every week since enrolling me in the local branch of the Scottish National Party in 1959, but this was a special visit. "We want you to stand in the by-election" was the message, so I'll always remember that 'flu; it marked a watershed. I gave up smoking, and I took up politics; how could I possibly have refused his request when I'd been reliving the spirit of Scotland in the writings of Lewis Grassic Gibbon?

Who were the leading campaigners in West Lothian in 1962? The first Constituency Committee consisted of Robert Kerr, Torphichen, draughtsman; John Hamilton, Westfield, paper mill worker; Jack Marshall, Bathgate, salesman; Danny McDonald, Westfield, paper mill worker; Angus McGillveray, East Whitburn, painter and decorator; Peter Rankine, Armadale, merchant seaman; Willie Kellock, Bo'ness, bank teller; Willie Ross, Bo'ness, jeweller and watchmaker; Clem Sim, Bathgate, steel

10

mill worker; Charlie Auld, Bo'ness, publican; Bill Robertson, Whitburn, apprentice surveyor; Harry Constable, Bo'ness, clerk; and as contact man for the Edinburgh University Nationalist Club, Donald Stevenson, student.

There wasn't a seasoned politician among us, but we were convinced that the political route we had chosen was the best for the people of Scotland. We attracted lots of support from ordinary people like ourselves who wanted a parliament re-established in Scotland, believing that the Scots could effectively solve their own problems far better than the English parliament in London, which so clearly neglected Scottish needs and wishes. We recruited many young people and made up in enthusiasm and dedication for what we lacked in experience and skill.

Into our midst in May came the SNP's first full-time organiser, Ian Macdonald. Ian had farmed in Ayrshire, and had been the SNP candidate in the Bridgeton by-election of 1961. With election agent Alan Niven he had run a campaign on a shoe-string with a handful of people and taken the SNP vote to over 18%. The result and the experience gained in Bridgeton convinced Ian Macdonald that the fight for self-government could definitely be won, and what the Party needed most of all to start an effective and national campaign was a full-time organiser. Ian decided to throw himself into full-time work for the Party and with no contract, and no promise of a salary, he gave up his farm at the term day in May and came through to Bathgate.

For 30 years West Lothian had returned Labour M.P.s with solid majorities. The county had been first won for Labour by Emanuel Shinwell in a by-election in 1928. He lost the seat at the succeeding General Election to a titled Tory land owner from a mining area. However, this aberration was corrected when the baronet in turn was defeated and George Mathers was elected, a quiet orthodox Labour Party man with trade union experience. His successor, John Taylor, was a man in the same style, who held the seat in 1959 with a majority of nearly 10,000.

Although the Labour Party apparently had it so easy in West Lothian, they had the reputation of having one of the best electoral machines in Scotland, and the electorate of West Lothian was accustomed to strong campaigning even if the result was a foregone conclusion. However, the pattern of both Tory and Labour campaigns had hardly changed in thirty years, and by 1962 the Labour Party leaders took their votes for granted. Certainly, in the early days of the campaign following John Taylor's death, few in West Lothian, and probably no one outside the county, doubted that the usual pulling of strings by party officials, accompanied by the customary doctrinaire mouthings of worn-out phrases which had once reflected genuine need, would bring the electorate into the polling booths ready to act on their time-honoured tendencies to ignore everything but the thoroughly respectable trustees of the British left and the British right.

However, West Lothian was to provide some surprises. Fortuitously, the stage had been set in February, at least in the columns of the *West Lothian Courier,* one of the County's two papers, as a result of a criticism by the *Courier* of a well-known SNP activist in Bathgate, James Moffat.

In a letter which I wrote to the *West Lothian Courier* on 21st February 1962, I defended James Moffat's suggestion that the Burghs of Bathgate, Armadale and Whitburn should join together along with the neighbouring landward areas, to form a new large burgh. The sense of Mr Moffat's proposals has been adequately corroborated by opinion and event long after his prophecy was made. To the *Courier's* editor I wrote that I did not see "that it is inconsistent to advocate centralisation for an area of ten or twenty square miles inhabited by communities with closely tied common interests and at the same time to advocate de-centralisation for Scotland which is from three hundred and fifty to eight hundred miles from the seat of Government and is inhabited by a separate nation with its own history and traditions, outlook and economy." I continued by agreeing that "extreme nationalism is a dangerous thing, if by that your reporter means the fascism which gives nations a 'master race' complex, but there is surely no sign of such an attitude in Scotland. The best defence against such dangers is the attitude of the Scottish people, the descendants of those who founded Western European democracy's first home. Scotland can be a self-governing nation again with no loss to herself or the world, and her size is no barrier. There are many independent economically healthy nations with much smaller populations and much smaller national incomes per head than Scotland. Less than one hundred years ago," I continued, "Scotland was the wealthiest nation in the world. The decline in the Scottish economy dates back to the 1914-18 War, the real beginning of heavy taxation, vast Government spending, and Government control of the economy. London Governments always think in terms of the U.K. economy. We in Scotland are only ten per cent of that economy, so we are relatively unimportant."

That re-statement of one classic view of those who wanted to end the Union with England was the forerunner of a spate of SNP propaganda such as had never been seen in one constituency before. We believed in the great message we had to give to the people of Scotland and we spared neither effort nor expense, in relation to our means, to get the message across. No one, apart from members of the SNP and a few supporters, thought that we would even save our deposit, as around five thousand votes were needed to do that.

We started putting propaganda advertisements in the local papers at the end of March, telling the people facts about unemployment and the continuing subsidy of England by Scotland. Then the Tory Government took a hand by withdrawing the 1s 3d per gallon preference on hydrocarbon oils which allowed the Scottish shale industry to continue in existence. It always seemed crazy to me that a Government should tax raw materials produced from its own natural resources in order to deny its own workers and industry any advantage over workers and companies in similar industries abroad. I now had a chance to campaign on the subject.

My first public meeting was within the shale oil district on Wednesday, 4th April 1962, in the village of Dechmont, between Bathgate and Broxburn. I called the Government's action against the Scottish shale oil industry "social and economic murder," and both local papers made that phrase my first headlines. Among the points I made were that there was enough raw material for profitable working for eighty years, according to the Managing Director of Scottish Oils Ltd., and yet, to satisfy foreign interests, the Government had decided to kill the industry stone dead at a time when unemployment was higher in West Lothian than it had been before the huge B.M.C. project had come to the county in the preceding year.

In fact, at this time over one thousand people, almost entirely men, were employed in the shale oil industry in the Lothians and an almost equivalent number of coal miners were employed supplying the oil industry with coal. At Dechmont, I pointed out that the Scottish shale oil industry was practically a nationalised industry as it was owned by the B.P. group of which the government had virtual control. The annual tax with which the Government was murdering this industry, throwing thousands of

13

people in the Lothians into uncertainty and despair, had been less than £1 million in recent years. I pointed out that most British manufacturing industry had the protection of a tariff. Why not protect a vital and important industry such as the shale oil industry with an assured future, if only by allowing duty exemption?

There is no doubt that Scottish oil was an important economic factor in West Lothian politics in 1962. There is even less doubt that Scottish oil of a different kind is the most significant economic factor in the politics of the whole of Scotland in 1973.

Another subject of importance in 1962 was the proposed British entry into the Common Market. Our by-election campaign in 1962 was the SNP's first opportunity to campaign in public on a fairly large scale against entry into the E.E.C. I have no doubt that our arguments against entry into the Common Market gained us some of our by-election support; but no one could have voted for me in West Lothian in June 1962, or in any later election, without realising that they were voting, above all, for self-government for Scotland.

At a meeting on a Sunday afternoon early in the campaign in Willie Kellock's dining room, which had the appearance of being more of a political command post than a domestic apartment, I suggested the slogan "Put Scotland First." Whether it was an original thought in my head or not, I cannot rightly tell, but years afterwards I came across a *Scots Independent* published during the Kilmarnock by-election of 1946 in which George Dott was the S.N.P. candidate. The slogan of his campaign had been "Put Scotland First."

As most Scottish readers will know, that slogan stood us in good stead. To some, it appears selfish, but like many other words and slogans in public use it is capable of more than one interpretation. However, in the simplest of terms, what we mean by "Put Scotland First" is "Set your own house in order before attending to other things"; and in the minds of the majority of the people of Scotland of 1973, as in 1962, there is no doubt that the management of the social and economic affairs of Scotland badly needs to be set in order. It has always been clear to the SNP that the first priority is the attainment of self-government; not that having a Parliament in Scotland is going to work a miracle overnight, but self-government will enable us to do things for ourselves in our own way with our own resources and without having to argue our case in a Parliament where Scotland's M.P.s are outnumbered eight to one.

To the SNP in 1962 and to nearly ten thousand voters in West Lothian, "Put Scotland First" was logical enough to be worthy of support; and that kind of support spread throughout Scotland until, at the 1970 General Election, more than 300,000 people voted to "Put Scotland First." Only eleven years earlier, in the General Election of 1959, the total SNP vote had been only 21,000.

Being runner-up in the by-election brought the Party more publicity than it had had for many years. The result was front-page news not only in all the Scottish dailies, but in England and the U.S.A. and in many other countries as well. It was not always the SNP position, nor its vote of 9,750, which was featured; in fact the B.B.C. did not mention the SNP vote in most of their bulletins—they, along with some Press commentators, considered the first loss of a Tory deposit in Scotland for forty-two years to be of more significance. The fact that the Liberal also lost his deposit quite unexpectedly, judging by repeated Liberal forecasts of "coming second with 15,000 votes," was also an important news item to some. In fact, the only significant aspect of the result was the size of the SNP vote.

There were now several interesting related subjects within my view, which had not been there four months earlier. The SNP had "arrived" in West Lothian and there was clearly going to be a lot of work ahead in organising the Party in the constituency in preparation for the General Election which had to be held before the end of October 1964. The by-election campaign had started with two branches—one serving the neighbouring villages of Westfield and Torphichen and the other serving the rest of West Lothian. An *ad hoc* Constituency Association had been formed to fight the by-election. I discovered after the campaign that the Party did not have any constitutional arrangements for Constituency Associations, so the drafting of a constitution was one of the top priorities for the SNP in West Lothian. It was clear that we had sufficient voting support and active members to form independent branches in at least half a dozen places. At a meeting of members in the county, held in Bathgate on 16th August 1962, about forty people attended from Whitburn, Fauldhouse, Broxburn, Winchburgh, Blackburn, Armadale, Bo'ness, Bridgend and Linlithgow, as well as from Westfield and Torphichen. Enthusiasm and determination were in the air.

There was also some lunacy. I was to learn in later years that each time the SNP makes some significant progress, the publicity attracts a few people who are violent and impatient

15

and devoid of any respect for democracy. At this Bathgate meeting, one man, a stranger to the rest of us, exhorted us to choose the road of violence and what he, and others, call "action" (as if democrats lie in their beds throughout election campaigns!). He was politely but firmly shown the door and I have never seen him since at an SNP meeting.

At that meeting, proposals for the Constituency Association constitution were discussed and arrangements made for a committee to draw up such a constitution. The meeting also dealt with such practical matters as having a common procedure for canvassing for new members and the holding of county training conferences for persons keen to become active representatives of the Party. There was a great deal to be done, and I was happily involved in helping with some of the organisational problems which arose after the spectacular growth of support for, and membership of, the Party in West Lothian.

The ten thousand votes the SNP had gained in West Lothian did not come from people who had suddenly changed their minds; what had changed was that for the first time in their lives these people had been given an opportunity to vote for a vigorous and responsible Scottish party which based its policy and philosophy on the truth that "Freedom is a noble thing." The result had reverberations outside West Lothian, particularly within the Scottish National Party, and in my own life; in contrast with having been previously uninvolved, I was now very conscious of various needs, and of ways in which I wanted to help promote the growth of the Party.

I first met the Party Chairman, Arthur Donaldson, when he came to speak in support of my candidature in the final stages of the campaign. I had a letter from him written in typical prophetic vein on 8th June, six days before polling. He wrote, "The Executive of the National Party, having considered the excellent results already showing from the West Lothian by-election, has decided that they offer every encouragement for mounting at the next General Election the biggest campaign we have ever attempted. May I even before the West Lothian poll convey the thanks and congratulations of the whole Party for the grand fight you have made? It will be an inspiration to our organisation in every constituency."

This was a great encouragement to us in West Lothian, and it was an accurate assessment of how we were progressing in the by-election campaign; the result certainly gave the Party the impetus it needed for steady growth, which continued virtually unabated for six years, until there was an organisation in every constituency in the land. When Arthur Donaldson made his prophecy in 1962, there were fewer than twenty active branches in the Party, and not one single constituency association.

As I became acquainted with Arthur Donaldson, I learned that he was one of the small band of dedicated people whose importance to the survival of the Scottish National Party in its very difficult years, which I judge to be from the mid-thirties until the late-fifties, had been supreme. As he put it to me some years later, there had been a time when all the activists of the SNP could have been the complement of a small passenger aircraft, and had they flown together and crashed without survivors, the cause of independence would have been lost to view for many years.

Freedom, as an indivisible ideal in all its aspects, was not the prerogative of the SNP in Scotland then, nor is it now, but the SNP has always been the only political party in Scotland to see that, if there is a nation called Scotland, then the freedom of independence is essential to its survival. As I said at the 1972 conference of the Party, "It is for the SNP to play a vital rôle in educating the Scottish public to realise that Scottish independence means other freedoms as well. It means freedom from the provincial second-class status in which the Labour and Tory Parties want to keep us. It means freedom from the cultural and social stereotypes imposed on us by the imperialistic past with which the English are so obsessed. It means freedom to express ourselves and to act as we ourselves decide. It means freedom to be a nation again."

It was impossible for me to avoid becoming involved at national level in the Party after the by-election. I not only saw what was needed in West Lothian in the way of organisation, I realised that the burden at national level had been carried by very few people, and during the election campaign I had learned many lessons about what the Party needed to do in the 1960s to win votes and members; and I had a fresh mind, free of any memories of the hard times the Party had gone through.

In my by-election campaign in 1962, I treated my audiences, and the electorate generally, as patriotic Scots looking for a solution to their community problems and to Scotland's problems in a political way that was honourable and likely to be effective. I always assumed that they believed in the continued existence of the nation. I dealt at length with economic matters and avoided "left versus right" arguments.

I did what fact-finding I could and used all the statistics I thought were applicable, particularly on employment and industrial development opportunities, and particularly comparing the expansion of the English economy with the unnatural decline of the Scottish economy.

At the first meeting of National Council after the by-election, on 7th July, I attended as an elected member. At that meeting, I learned for the first time what the democratic support of a comparatively massive vote can do for a person in the eyes of others. Although unknown to all but two of the persons attending that Council meeting, apart from being the man who had 9,750 votes in West Lothian, I was appointed Convener of the Party's Economics Committee, a member of the Party's National Executive Committee, and a member of the Election Committee which is responsible for interviewing and assessing the members nominated as possible Parliamentary candidates; and I was authorised to issue statements to the Press on the subject of the Scottish Economy. It seemed to me that I had served a very short apprenticeship before being given so much responsibility. In fact, it was a reflection of the small size of the Party and of the limited number of people available for the huge task the Party had undertaken.

I clearly remember the lack of authoritarianism in these meetings, which gave me my first impressions of the leadership of the Party in action. I was very conscious of power being held in trust and of decisions being reached by consensus, and of an active participating interest in all that was going on; and throughout all, I was aware of the great faith of this small group of men and women. They and their predecessors, in relation to the nation a tiny group, had laboured lovingly and long, seeing only the slightest flicker of life in what some observers thought was a corpse. They had also seen division of effort such as the Covenant campaign of the late '40s and early '50s in which over two million people signed a document pledging support for a Scottish Parliament. I had taken enthusiastic part in that campaign after signing the principal document in the Assembly Hall in Edinburgh. Such efforts had revived nationalism but had channelled the rivers of enthusiasm into the almost stagnant canals of the main U.K. parties instead of creating a watercourse of united Scottish political effort.

In fact, among the handful of people in Scotland who were the activists of the SNP in early 1962, the Bridgeton by-election of the previous autumn had shown that there was more than a flicker of life in the corpse, and many of these activists came to canvass the electorate of West Lothian and help in other ways. Among those from outside the Constituency who helped in 1962 and who are still active in the Party ten years later was Dr Robert McIntyre. He was the SNP's first M.P.. He was elected for Motherwell in a by-election in 1945, in a straight fight with a Labour Party candidate. The war-time coalition was in force, hence the absence of a Tory candidate. Between entering Parliament and the declaration of a General Election, Robert McIntyre had only twenty-one Parliamentary days, but in those few days he did more questioning for Scotland than any other M.P. had done in the ten years of that Parliament. When an English M.P. protested at his energetic activity, Dr McIntyre retorted, "I will never tire of pointing out to members of this House that if they do not want to hear more about Scotland, they have the solution in their own hands. I do not want to be here any more than they want to listen to me here; I want to be elsewhere, in an Assembly directly responsible to the Scottish people."

His election saved Prestwick Airport from the demise arranged for it by the Ministry of Aviation because it threatened to compete with London. He asked numerous questions and showed the abilities of an incisive and astute politician which have been of such value to the SNP for so long.

At the General Election of 1945, he was in a three-cornered contest and the seat was lost. In 1945, the SNP's rules had permitted members to be members of other political parties. The lesson of Motherwell was clear. People could not have two such loyalties, so the rules were changed and since then members of the SNP have undertaken not to be members of any other political party. Members can be and are socialist, conservative or liberal, but their prime concern is self-government. and they believe in achieving that aim first.

Mrs Mary Dott, who had been Secretary of the Party in the late 40s, spoke at one of my first meetings—that in Broxburn on 18th April—making the headlines with the phrase "Scottish M.P.s are spineless." Mrs Dott had been one of the early members of the original National Party of Scotland in 1928. Her belief in seeking the democratic support of the electorate for self-government had never wavered.

In her speech at Broxburn in 1962, Mrs Dott said that the Scottish M.P.s at Westminster were "afraid of being laughed at in London and ashamed of their nationality." She compared them with "the men of real character who had been Scots first in their representation of their constituencies—Tom Johnston, James Maxton, Walter Elliot and many others—Buchan, Wheatley, Horne—they all had some Scottish vigour and enthusiasm which was lacking in our Scottish M.P.s today." I doubt if any observer of the Scottish political scene eleven years later would find much more Scottish vigour among Scotland's Labour and Tory M.P.s than Mrs Dott found in 1962.

The by-election gave me my first introduction to Radio Free Scotland and to Gordon Wilson, a young lawyer who was Director of Programmes. Along with Frank Thompson, the P.R.O. for the organisation, and a regular band of helpers, Gordon Wilson pushed R.F.S. and the case for self-government into the columns of the newspapers in a very effective way. Two years later he became National Secretary of the Party, a post he held for seven years, giving invaluable service to the Party and to Scotland.

To the vast majority of Party workers in 1962 I was an absolute newcomer to the SNP. Another recruit was Mrs Rosemary Hall, whom I had known for fifteen years without realising she was a nationalist. We had both been on the staff of a C.A. firm and also involved in the running of the *Saltire Review*. As she was one of the most capable and nicest people I had ever known, I was delighted that she should join the SNP. Once she had finished her work with the C.A. Institute in 1964, she became totally involved in the work of the Party, in which she is now National Secretary.

The arguments used by the five candidates and their supporting speakers in the West Lothian by-election were on classical party lines. The principal and the most significant difference between this contest and almost all other previous electoral contests in Scotland, either in by-elections or General Elections, was the fact that the Scottish National Party took full advantage of its very unusual equality of opportunity.

The by-election evoked little or no interest outside the boundaries of West Lothian. The daily Press, radio and TV paid scant attention to it and therefore exercised no direct influence on the thinking of the voters. The absence of influence from these powerful media helped to make for equality of opportunity, a factor of great importance, particularly to the Communist, Liberal and S.N.P. candidates who are invariably at a disadvantage. In 1962 the SNP was virtually denied any access at all to television or radio and it was treated as a joke by the press, so the chance of being interviewed on a by-election TV programme, on a basis of equality with the other candidates, was most welcome.

In the two county weekly papers, the SNP also had an equal opportunity with the other contesting parties. Although the editorial view of both papers has not been favourable to the SNP, they have been fair in their allocation of space, especially during Parliamentary Elections. In addition to reports of meetings in the papers, the SNP embarked on an unprecedented advertising campaign which, I am sure, helped to win us support. Our adverts, like my speeches, were almost entirely concerned with the economic and social evidence in favour of self-government.

We had the shale oil industry as a prime topic, an industry which once employed 12,000 people in the Lothians. Over and over again, I tried to convince the people that the shale oil industry did not have a subsidy as the *Courier* and many other people tried to make out. What the shale oil industry had was a *burden* of Government duty, one which was more than the industry could bear. It would have been a profitable industry had there been no such duty to pay.

In my argument I quoted a whole list of manufactured items which had the protection of an import duty. I argued, "Why not oil? The oil industry in the Lothians has been sacrificed to interests outside of Scotland and outside the U.K. The Labour M.P.s interested in the industry have lobbied for years with no result whatsoever. Do you believe that a Scottish government, no matter what political opinion it held, would have closed down an industry which it owned? (for the U.K. Government controlled the Scottish oil industry).

"This closure," I said, "shows the weakness of Scotland's position without a Government of its own and shows that only lip service is paid to Scotland's needs by the three English-dominated political parties, and by the Trade Union movement in Scotland."

Speaking in my support at a meeting described in both local papers as "the largest political meeting to be held in Bathgate for many years," under the chairmanship of Mr Peter Fletcher, J.P., President of Bathgate Co-operative Society, Robert McIntyre accurately summed up the SNP view as follows: "The body blows now being suffered by our economy in Scotland are the direct result of the deliberate policy of trying to fit Scotland's economy into an English strait-jacket. They are not

21

the result of any basic lack of materials or skill of which we have a good average share. They are the result of the political subversion of our national community. It does not matter which of the recent disasters you care to choose, you will find that political decisions taken in London are responsible. For these decisions the London political parties are all jointly responsible.

"Take shale. This industry which is the pioneer oil industry of the world was built up before London started putting its nose into Scottish economic affairs. It is now taxed out of existence; a tax begun by a Liberal Government and continued by a Labour Government and extended by a Tory Government. They have all treated English industry differently with protective tariffs and so on. Here is a clear case of a political decision made in London directly and adversely affecting Scotland."

Coal was another important topic during the by-election, especially as there were six pits operating in the county at the time. On the whole, we were treated with indifference at the pit-heads in 1962, mainly because of lack of understanding of the outlook of the S.N.P. This was not surprising as, like most industrial workers in Scotland, the miners' only source of information about the SNP was the anti-SNP propaganda of Labour Party and Communist Party activists. I recall being at one colliery where a huge miner came up to me, looked me up and down, spat in my face, and with the liberal use of a four-letter word, informed me he was a pillar of the Labour Party, and told me where to go.

After the by-election, I seriously considered seeking a job with the N.C.B. in order to identify more closely with the mining community which I realised had been exploited for generations to a greater extent than other sections of the working class. However, I sensed that I was about ten years late in thinking about it and that I would be less than honest with myself if I made such a move.

The coal industry in Scotland was one of the main subjects in the speeches of the Communist candidate, Gordon MacLennan, the most accomplished politician and the best speaker of the five candidates in the by-election. The Labour candidate was Mr Tam Dalyell of The Binns. As a socialist aristocrat, he was an unusual political activist.

The Labour Party totally ignored the possibility that the SNP would gain a significant number of votes in this by-election, until the last few days when they realised, to their astonishment, that the SNP would come second with about ten thousand votes. The Tories also totally ignored the SNP in the by-election. I remember meeting Mr James Kidd, a Linlithgow lawyer whom I knew, one of the leading lights in the Tory Party in West Lothian, on polling day. Their organisation in West Lothian being hopeless, they could be excused, I suppose, for thinking, at even that late hour, that they were still in second place and that I would lose my deposit. James Kidd greeted with scorn and laughter my forecast that I would be given about 10,000 votes and come second. He, and countless others, had to take a different view of things twenty-four hours later.

In the by-election, the Tories still fought as "Unionists." Their stated policy was one with which I had little sympathy. It was "to defend the Government's policy and to attack the policies of the Labour and Liberal Parties." That was the total message. Is it unkind to say that it was typically Tory?

Three nights before Polling Day I went to heckle the Secretary of State for Scotland. The Government's head man in Scotland at the time was Mr John Maclay. He addressed a meeting of about forty in Linlithgow. More than half of the audience were nationalists.

With the help of David Murray, an industrial journalist and a leading writer on steel and coal, I had examined on the previous evening the recently-published annual accounts of the N.C.B. for 1961. The Scottish Division had been "exposed" as having lost £19 million but, on studying the accounts and comparing them with the accounts for earlier years, I discovered major differences in presentation which made my C.A. hackles as well as my Scottish hackles rise.

I asked Mr Maclay why these changes had been made. He replied that as N.C.B. accounts were not a Parliamentary responsibility he could not answer. I was allowed a "supplementary" and pointed out that in the accounts, which I had in my hand, were the words, "published by authority of Parliament on 30th May 1962." Surely Mr Maclay should be able to answer?

Mr Maclay was very gentlemanly but protested that he would need a Chartered Accountant to help him answer my question. So I leapt to my feet a third time and offered my services. As he was about the only person in the meeting who did not know who I was he could not understand why everybody laughed so loudly until the Tory chairman whispered in his ear that I was not only a C.A. but also the SNP candidate.

Naturally I made what capital I could of the NCB accounts —how I wished that I'd had the facts a few days earlier. The next night in Bo'ness I said, "The public in general and the rank and file of the coal industry in particular have been grossly misled by the report of a £19 million loss in the N.C.B.'s Scottish Division in 1961. The accounts published by authority of Parliament on 30th May of this year contain interest charges of nearly £6 million against the Scottish Division. This charge never appeared in any previous accounts and its inclusion without any note or word of explanation is definitely misleading.

"Moreover, the accounts for 1962 do not include certain comparative figures which appeared in the published accounts for 1961 and previous years. Had these not been omitted, it would have been obvious to the Press and the public that a vitally important change in accounting procedure had been made. In fact, the financial results for 1961 were no worse than those for 1959.

"Why has this change been made?" I asked. "Why could Scottish Secretary of State John Maclay not answer this question when I put it to him in Linlithgow last night? Because the N.C.B. headquarters in London, with chairman Lord Robens as the ringleader, and the Government, have deliberately set out to create misgivings among the general public in Scotland and to stultify further the growth of industrial Scotland.

"These hypocrites say how sorry they are when thousands of Scots have to leave their homes and the communities in which they have lived and loved to seek work in England. They actually tell our miners to go to England.

"London Government killed the shale oil industry. Unless you, the people of Scotland, do something about it now, there will be another death in the Scottish industrial family—the coal industry."

In our propaganda, as in my speeches throughout the campaign, we presented hard facts to instil confidence in the idea of Scotland being self-governed. We publicised how badly governed we were from London, and in an advertisement we pointed out the following:

"Your chance of a new job in Scotland, compared with your chance in England—6 to 1 against (new jobs in ten years, 1951-1961: Scotland 1·5% decrease, minus 34,000; England 9% increase, plus 1,678,000).

"Your chance of unemployment in Scotland compared with your chance in England—5 to 2 on—(unemployment rate in Scotland is consistently two and a half times that in England)."

We advertised "Scotland's Balance Sheet" highlighting the

taxation subsidy from Scotland to England, and we advertised "Scotland, the rich partner," showing that Scottish dollar exports were five times, per head of population, the dollar exports from England and Wales.

In summing up the result immediately after the by-election, I claimed that it "was fair reward for hard work, enthusiasm and faith in Scotland and the Scottish people." Eleven years after that election, I am still of the same opinion. The by-election campaign had made me more convinced than ever "that the Tory Government and the other U.K. Parties and the U.K. Unions cared nothing for Scotland except as a Province of the U.K. and that they were bent on destroying Scotland, consciously or otherwise." I forecast "that the National Party was well on the way to becoming Scotland's second Party, and not only in West Lothian." Six years later, in fact, the SNP was, in the Municipal Elections of 1968, Scotland's *first* Party, getting a bigger share of votes than any other Party. Voting patterns in Municipal and County Council Elections vary from those in General Elections but the 1968 vote is a clear and encouraging indication of what is possible for the SNP. What I did not forecast in June 1962 was the effect on my own life and outlook which my political commitment would bring in the years ahead.

CHAPTER 3

DISCOVERING THE SNP, 1962-64

ROMANTIC SCOTTISH patriotism has hardly held my interest as an object in itself since the age of eleven or twelve. It certainly was well and truly imprinted on my mind and in my heart both at home and throughout my primary schooling in Bathgate. It is part of me and I value its ineradicable influence which contributes to my outlook as a Scot, but it forms little or no part of my expressed argument for self-government. As a child, I was simply Scottish, and proud of it. As I grew to manhood, I had no idea at all of Scotland having any kind of inferiority in relation to England, except in size, and I accepted what I then looked on as a partnership between Scotland and England.

After five years in the army, spent almost entirely in the company of Englishmen in England or overseas, I was, to some people, apparently quite anglicised. But it was only superficial and after demobilisation a chain of fortuitous circumstances led me to learn much about Scottish culture and tradition which I had not heard in secondary school nor since leaving it, and my English acquirements quickly disappeared. That experience taught me to understand how Scots out of Scotland identify with the communities in which they are prepared to settle down. They forget Scotland, except as an acceptable romantic notion.

Mainly through reading, which was stimulated by activity in the Saltire Society. I greatly improved my knowledge of my own country. Clearly what can be seen in the present sickness of Scotland is the incredible concentration of Scottish educationalists on imparting knowledge of England to Scottish children at the expense of knowledge of Scotland. I now believe that the only cure for that sickness is a political one. However, in the late forties and early fifties I found much satisfaction in the work of the Saltire Society, particularly in its Publications Committee.

In the immediate post-war period, the Committee embarked successfully on a varied programme of worthwhile publishing—classics, modern poets, chapbooks and booklets on current aspects of Scottish life. Other subjects such as the songs of Francis George Scott were dealt with; and from 1954 - 61 it published *The Saltire Review of Arts, Letters and Life*.

However, as the years passed and the Saltire Society, the National Trust, the Covenant Association and many other more specialised organisations seemed to me to be making very little progress in the creative evolution of society in Scotland, I began to have serious doubts about the continuance of Scotland if we were to depend on such bodies, not only to cherish the best of the past but to nourish new growth for the future. They preserved much of great value and they encouraged some new growth, but it was inadequate in comparison with the great weight of English and U.S.A. culture which tended to suffocate and supplant Scottishness.

So, in 1959, I decided that only in the political field would Scotland find herself a nation again. After reading what was sent to me by the five political parties active in Scotland, I joined the Scottish National Party, convinced by the facts of Scotland's decline in the 1950s and by the logic of the double contention that if there is a nation of Scots it is entitled to self-government, and that if the people of Scotland do not achieve self-government, the nation of Scots will disappear as a living regenerating community.

For years I had considered myself as good a Scot as my neighbour, living and working in Scotland by choice and taking an active part in the social, cultural and religious life of the community in which I lived, and in several national bodies concerned with social and cultural affairs. For at least fifteen years I had believed in self-government for Scotland but I had done nothing practical about it. 1962 showed me that the only realistic effort towards self-government is to persuade other Scots to believe in it and vote for it in local and parliamentary Elections.

For the past 25 years at least, the people of Scotland have shown in plebiscites, Gallup Polls and opinion surveys that 75 to 80 per cent of them are in favour of self-government for Scotland. To turn that vision of self-government into an effective elected Scottish Parliament requires, in essence, no more than a massive vote for a party which is capable of negotiating with Westminster and of setting up a democratic parliament within a constitution acceptable to the majority of the people of Scotland.

The activities and the comparative success of the SNP in the West Lothian by-election convinced me of the certainty of self-government if the Scottish National Party could gain the confidence of the people of Scotland and secure that massive vote. We needed recruitment; we needed money; we needed

27

political training and experience; we needed electoral organisation and we needed vision, imagination, courage and knowledge in order to gain the confidence of our fellow Scots. One of the things of which I became convinced during the by-election campaign was the need to engage in political dialogue, with knowledge and conviction, on almost any current topic with political implications. To me this meant that the Scottish National Party had to become conversant with all that was going on in Scotland. It was no use expressing pious hopes in committee meetings or pamphlets without getting out and about among the folk, identifying with their needs and aspirations here and now. Certainly we had to promote a new vision of the Scotland we were seeking but we could not hope to get support for it without showing a clear path leading to it from present-day Scotland.

The SNP policy document which we had used in the 1962 by-election had been drafted in 1947. It was a sound document but it needed to be updated and I determined in 1962 that I would make it one of my priorities to have, if possible, such a policy document ready for the forthcoming General Election.

One of the aspects of this work was the collection of data. At that time the economic and social facts available from government and other sources were quite inadequate, and it was clear to some of us in the SNP that something had to be done immediately to remedy the situation. On 30th June 1962, David Rollo from Kirkintilloch, the Party Treasurer, wrote to me asking: "Would it be possible for the SNP to sponsor an organisation for economic research which could then write to firms and individuals under this name for information regarding such things as exports and so on? The various bodies would be more likely to reply to this non-political organisation than to the SNP. There is a Scottish Economic Society but it acts rather like an undertaker as far as Scotland is concerned. The disadvantages are: dissipation of effort and lack of manpower. Do you think we could do anything without involving already active members in more work?"

Well, we tried. Later in the year, at a meeting in Linlithgow, the "Social and Economic Inquiry Society of Scotland" was founded. Its original members were not all members of the SNP, indeed they were not all nationalists and included the well-known journalist, Andrew Hargrave (whom I had first met when he called to interview me during the by-election). He was a member of the Labour Party. There were other prominent journalists such as David Murray and David Donald, then editor

28

of the Scottish Council's magazine *Scotland*. The Scottish Council's Manager, John Donachy, also joined. Another founder member was Michael Starforth, then Treasurer of the Scottish Liberal Party. He had been a nationalist since his youth but, like many others, had believed in the 1950s that support of the Scottish Liberal Party was the best route to choose to self-government. However, he later became disillusioned and he left the Liberals and joined the Scottish National Party. Others who took an interest in the foundation of SEISS were Dr R. Maclagan Gorrie, a retired forester and land use consultant who had spent many years in Asia and who was, in 1962, actively involved in the Highland Fund, the Saltire Society and the Royal Scottish Forestry Society; Lawrence Daly, of the N.U.M., of which he is now the General Secretary; George Brodlie, who is now Financial Editor of *The Scotsman*; Dr John Highet, then lecturer in Sociology at Glasgow University; and a most remarkable man then in his eighties, John Dow, who had been County Assessor of Dumfriesshire for over ten years after retiring as a Chief Inspector of Taxes.

Following the by-election, Mr Dow had engaged in a correspondence with me which, from my point of view, was one of the most fruitful in which I ever took part. He was a man of great ability who had all his life believed in the need for self-government for Scotland. The novelist, Dr Neil Gunn had been a junior in an Excise office with him in the early years of this century and I guess that the young man who was later to be such a successful writer had some mutual understanding with his older colleague who was to spend such a long life in the public service. Mr Dow, later in the '60s, wrote a regular series for the *Scots Independent* envisaging how things might be run in a free Scotland.

In accordance with David Rollo's original idea, we hoped to attract into the active ranks of SEISS people who were not already fully committed to work within the Scottish National Party. However, the Press, particularly the *Glasgow Herald*, unfairly labelled us an SNP organisation when we announced the formation of the Society and discouraged other people from joining. Although it did some excellent work, which the SNP could not have done, by 1966 it was run entirely by SNP activists and the pressure of Party work and involvement made it temporarily superfluous. The situation is different today and most Scottish Universities have members of staff who are actively interested in the social and economic state of Scotland

—there were hardly any such people in 1962, as the SEISS surveys of 1963 showed—and SEISS is being revived today quite independently of the SNP and on the non-party basis originally envisaged. I looked on SEISS as a source of facts and of authority and as a goad for prodding people in Scotland's universities to look at Scottish problems. It did not in any way take over the responsibilities of the SNP to study the economic situation in Scotland, to educate its members on that situation and to propose ways and means of dealing with it politically.

During what was left of 1962, and throughout 1963 and 1964, I sought constantly to activate people to help with the Economics Committee which was my appointed sphere of activity within the Party at national level. By the end of 1962 I had been successful in only one direction—we published a useful fuel policy dealing mainly with coal. This had been produced following some instructive and entertaining meetings which I convened, gathering a mixed assortment of people on each occasion. I can well remember a fierce argument in a Linlithgow café in which David Murray stood up and argued fiercely across the table with Tam MacDonald, a miner from Armadale. Tam also stood up, with one foot on his chair, and they almost came to blows. I also had the benefit of discussions with management executives in the N.C.B. and with N.U.M. officials and I visited several collieries and talked to many miners.

The result was a clear picture of the state of the industry which we then had to consider in terms of the country's needs.

A policy statement was drawn up, approved by the Party, and published in February 1963 as *Room for improvement—The Scottish National Party's answer for coal.* It was a report and a policy with "comment on the management control of the industry since British nationalisation in 1947."

Coal tends to be forgotten as I write this book but it must not be forgotten. The coal industry in Scotland need never have been allowed to decline so drastically and with such serious social upheavals as did occur. With a Scottish Parliament, it certainly would not have been criminally misdirected as it was under London control which tried to fit it into a grandiose plan for the United Kingdom.

Some points from our document of 1963 are worthy of quotation here. "A policy for the whole Scottish Coal Industry must be laid down by Government as part of an integrated fuel policy in order to ensure the best utilisation of national assets and to provide the cheapest possible source of fuel and power for industry. The actual management of the coal industry must be localised in the coalfields.

"The State is under obligation to direct the maximum improvement in working conditions in the coal industry and to be responsible for the social consequences of implementing a fuel policy which may lead to colliery closures. The Government must be responsible for providing work for miners who become redundant.

"Where the lack of alternative employment makes it morally and socially desirable or necessary for a particular colliery or particular collieries to be kept in operation, even although they are not profitable, the Government must accept responsibility for the operating loss on these collieries. The Scottish National Party holds that co-ordinated national planning for, and provision of, alternative employment is the responsibility of Government.

"A thorough geophysical and geological survey of Scotland must be made at the earliest possible opportunity to complement and add to the work already done in this connection. The Government should authorise this now."

These principles and objectives are still relevant in 1973.

The success of the coal leaflets spurred me on to try and deal with other economic affairs. Typical of the way in which I harangued the Party was a report I made to the Party's Annual Conference in May 1963.

"The immediate aim of this Party must be to enlist more and more support and therefore more and more votes until we have representation in the House of Commons in London. All our manpower, but particularly our skilled manpower, must be deployed with this immediate and important end in view; but what do we find? People, including myself, who have far too many interests absorbing their time and talents, to the detriment of their effort within and for the SNP, should pause and consider, and calculate the value in SNP votes of all they do outside their jobs and their private domestic lives. If all the committed one hundred per cent supporters of the Scottish National Party who have training, skill and aptitude or any of these things which could profitably serve the Economics Committee, made themselves available, then we could have a detailed policy inside weeks. As this is like crying for the moon, however, I have hope that the Branches and individual members will bombard

31

the Economics Committee with ideas and proposals of people who could be of use to the Committee and therefore to the Party.

"At this stage in its development this Party needs, in my view, a policy consisting mainly of clearly stated principles, but there are some vital issues affecting the lives of people or likely to affect them under a Scottish Government which should be stated in more detail. We have fairly detailed proposals for coal. Let us do more of this—but always remembering that as we develop as a Party, enlisting more and more support, these detailed policies will come in for close scrutiny and are quite likely to be the subjects of proposals for change; what I hope will happen is that the Scottish people will become actively concerned about the state of Scottish things *as* Scottish things and not merely as Scottish variations of U.K. or English things —to such an extent that they argue constructively over policy proposals for a modern and independent Scotland.

"It is absolutely essential for Scotland to have a Government with the authority of the Scottish people to carry out the following programme firmly, efficiently and speedily: —

"1. There must be a policy of full employment and pressure of demand on production and population. This requires a Government Department of Industrial Development and Research with power to induce development by offering substantial grants and loans to individuals and groups, including especially co-operatively-owned factory groups. This Government department must include a number of individuals quite free to travel and search for ideas and to channel them to men and women willing to develop them. The term "workshop factories" has been used elsewhere for such initial development which is absolutely essential in Scotland now.

"2. There must be a firm and all-embracing incomes policy operated not so much by Government as through the Government Treasury by a fully representative democratic constitution acceptable to all concerned, whether employers or employees. such a policy should also embody the measures proposed by the mature and unselfish social conscience which it should be the aim of Government to encourage and develop in the population.

"3. Investment on a grand scale in technical education to improve the efficiency of workers of all kinds, hence to improve industrial efficiency and increase productivity, while at the same time increasing human dignity by making it possible for more members of the community to contribute more to the development of the country's resources, trade and wealth and to its power to help less fortunate countries. This field of technical education should also include really adequate facilities for training men and women who, for one reason or another, require to change from one industry to another and have to learn skills and techniques quite new to them. Such investment on a bold scale would undoubtedly benefit the economy of Scotland and the whole population.

"These are matters of immediate concern and yet they can also be considered as applicable to an independent Scotland. Let us not think too much of that Promised Land. Let us fight for votes for Scotland *now* for our land is desperately needing us. Let us stir up our compatriots and awaken their conscience so that they will join us and forge a national determination for democratic independence. When we have done that, London Government of Scotland will be doomed."

All of these ideas were, later in the '60s, taken up by the Party, discussed in depth, argued over, and hammered into acceptable political policies with a common thread of the radical philosophy which has permeated Scottish politics and Scottish thought on government for centuries.

The reference to "co-operatively-owned factory groups" was partly inspired by the results of a chance meeting shortly after the by-election in 1962. I had taken a group of boys from Torphichen Kirk Sunday School to Iona, a place which I love to visit. I was a supporter of the Iona Community and had been, in certain respects, a follower of the Community's Founder, Dr George Macleod, for many years. My visit to Iona in 1962 was very brief but I met the deputy leader of the Iona Community, Ralph Morton, and we discussed, among other things, the need for justice and for the tempering of greed in a sophisticated industrial economy. He told me of a project, under discussion in a group sponsored by the Iona Community in Glasgow, for the setting up of a self-owned manufacturing company. I was very interested, and when I returned home I contacted the man leading the project, Tom McAlpine, an electrical engineer and Labour Party town councillor in Hamilton who was a lay member of the Iona Community. I was invited to join the working group, which I did, and I was eventually appointed an appeal trustee of the funds collected to set up Rowen Engineering Company Limited, and its share-holding organisation consisting of the workers in the Company, Rowen Community.

The working group consisted of socialists mainly, with one or two nationalists including Ken Reid, who had been associated with a co-operative building enterprise in Glasgow many years earlier. Most of the participants were members or supporters of CND, War on Want and kindred organisations. At least three of them have been recruited since to the ranks of SNP activists—Tom McAlpine himself, who is now Convener of the SNP's Industrial Development Committee; Isobel Lindsay (Tom's wife), now a lecturer in Sociology at Strathclyde University and an Executive Vice-Chairman of the SNP, in charge of Publicity matters; and Keith Bovey, a well-known Glasgow solicitor.

These three did not join the SNP for some years. When we met together in 1962 our common concern was getting a factory going. Rowen Engineering Company survives, but it now seems to Tom McAlpine and to me that its constitution was based rather too much on ideals and aspirations. It was launched quite openly as an experiment and I believe that the experience of the Rowen Community (named after Robert Owen, the great co-operative pioneer of New Lanark) will be of value in the development of a form of industrial democracy which will prove to be effective socially, economically and politically in the future.

In the course of searching out ideas and opinion with a possible bearing on the factory project, Tom McAlpine arranged for us to meet Richard Hauser, a practical sociologist with an international reputation who had scored some success in sorting out industrial strife and in the education of 14 - 15 year old children whom conventional educational methods had failed to reach. I count myself fortunate in having met Hauser. The influence of the meetings I had with him and the book which he and his wife, Hephzibah Menuhin, wrote, *The Fraternal Society,* came at a most opportune time and helped me to understand and express much that I had been thinking about.

In political terms, I rate the Hausers' book more important than any of the other ideological or intellectual influences on me at this time. I got a new vision of the world and I got a new vision of the possibilities of self-government for Scotland. I believed, since thinking about it many years before, that the Scots are essentially a fraternal people. I suspect that the threads of this outlook could go back to pre-Scottish Caledonia and that they were strengthened by Celtic influences from both Eire and from Wales. There are many well-known instances which reflect a collective fraternalism which has marked the Scottish people throughout their history.

The most recent example of this was the work-in on Clyde-side in 1971 - 72. Of course there are many political and materialist influences to consider in this remarkable show of initiative and solidarity. But the uncompromising fraternalism of it seems to me to have been so Scottish that I cannot imagine it happening elsewhere in the same way.

The Rowen Engineering experiment was not born out of a great emotional reaction of protest against a real situation involving whole communities, as was the U.C.S. work-in. Rowen's roots were almost entirely in idealism and it was brought to being by a few people who believed that they could see in their mind's eye a better form of industrial society than that which existed in Glasgow in the mid-twentieth century.

In the autumn of 1962, the Labour M.P. for West Lothian, Tam Dalyell, launched an appeal for a self-owned co-operative factory in West Lothian to combat unemployment. It provoked instant enthusiasm which was most encouraging, but it suffered almost instant failure not so much from lack of funds, because there was at least £5000 subscribed or promised in a matter of weeks, and that was more than Rowen Engineering started with, but because there was no committed and enthusiastic leadership available with the necessary knowledge, training, experience and outlook to run such an enterprise.

Both of these projects, however, were an indication, and a clear one, that the vast majority of the people will enthusiastically support the idea that some form of industrial democracy could end the bitterness of the warring factions of capitalism.

Rowen had one successful off-shoot, significantly in Wales. The Rowen Onllwyn Factory employs disabled miners manufacturing tubular furniture. To me it is no accident that the desire for experiment in industrial democracy in order to find a new formula, particularly for productive industry, should show itself in Scotland and in Wales. In both countries, the roots of this embryo movement are fraternal, whereas the origins of such factories as exist in England appear to be paternal and authoritarian, and rather more empirical than the developments in Wales and Scotland. The fraternal idealism which Robert Burns expressed in many immortal lines for the enjoyment of all humanity reflect a distinctive attitude which he found in many of his fellow Scots and in their traditions. I believe that he would find the same outlook among the Scots today.

After the by-election I spent a week with my family at St

Andrews. Eileen was seven, David was five and Sheila was nearly two. (Patrick did not arrive until the following February.) The novelty and excitement of the by-election had concealed from Maimie and me what "Put Scotland First" was going to mean in relation to our private family life in the years ahead. I had always had active outside interests, but taking part in the struggle for self-government was to become the most important thing in my life, to the almost total exclusion of other interests. My employment and my private life were certainly to change to accommodate my new responsibilities. In the summer of 1962, looking at Scotland and looking at the Scottish National Party, I saw clearly so many urgent things to be done that my first difficulty was in deciding which jobs to tackle first.

In 1962, Ian Macdonald, as National Organiser, was the ideal man for the job, with his irrepressible optimism and his ability to speak clearly and convincingly on the aims of the Party. Wherever and whenever he heard of interest in the Party, especially in areas without any previous record of SNP interest, he arranged for the distribution of literature and the holding of meetings and the formation of Branches. During his seven years as National Organiser, the Party practically doubled its strength each year.

We had another by-election on our hands in 1962, in the Glasgow constituency of Woodside, the SNP candidate being Alan Niven. The circumstances of this constituency were very different from those of West Lothian. It had been a marginal seat. The three English Parties took a strong anti-SNP line and I found the electorate in Glasgow much less receptive to our propaganda than the electorate of West Lothian. In the result the SNP gained twelve per cent. The Party was very disappointed, but worse was to come in the following year when the party had three by-elections on its hands at the one time—Kinross and West Perthshire, Dundee West and Dumfriesshire.

If the SNP had not had a few incurable optimists among its members it would have disappeared years ago. In Kinross and West Perthshire, where Arthur Donaldson had scored 15 per cent at the 1959 General Election, it was hoped that the vote would be increased. Certainly the response at meetings and in canvassing was quite encouraging but the vote fell to seven per cent. A fortnight later the same percentage was obtained by Dr James Lees in Dundee West and then, in early December 1963, John Gair, a local schoolmaster in Dumfriesshire, polled nearly ten per cent.

36

One of the main differences between the West Lothian campaign on the one hand and the Woodside campaign in November 1962 and the three campaigns in the late autumn of 1963 on the other was the fact that West Lothian received no attention from national news media until the result was declared. Particularly in Kinross and West Perthshire there was massive daily coverage for the U.K. parties, mainly, of course, for the Tory candidate, Sir Alec Douglas Home, who had shelved his peerage in order to become a commoner Prime Minister. The coverage, of course, was 99 per cent for the continuation of the rule of the English Establishment over Scotland. The SNP was against the rest and the rest had virtually all the means of mass communication on their side. That has been the case at most by-elections and General Elections since 1962.

Along with several others who helped in the three campaigns in 1963, I was very critical of the manner in which they were fought. I can recall a fairly tense meeting of the National Executive Committee in Dundee during the by-election there when I moved that the by-election in Dumfries should not be contested. I had put a lot of work into investigating the situation in Dumfries, including going there with a team from West Lothian to do an opinion survey, and I forecast that we would lose another deposit. I was disappointed that I could not find a seconder in the Executive for my motion not to contest.

However, a week or two later, after polling day in Dumfries, I wrote an article for the *Scots Independent* in which I admitted that "in view of the fact that John Gair finished less than five hundred votes (one per cent) behind the Liberal certainly justifies the decision to fight, in spite of the lost deposit." In that campaign there had been only three weeks of winter weather in which to work and the Party had started with a Branch in Dumfries, and not very much else, in what is a huge constituency.

An issue which assumed quite important proportions at this stage in the Party's history was how to deal with the Liberals. We had dealt with them fairly effectively in West Lothian, where we claimed that they had "intervened" as they had adopted a candidate although they had no organisation, after we had adopted a candidate for the by-election. However, in Glasgow Woodside, where they had a well-known candidate in the person of Jack House, a popular Glasgow journalist, and in Kinross and West Perthshire, where they had a local farmer as their candidate, the Liberals obtained significantly more votes than the SNP. The Liberals had not fought in Dundee West so we could make no comparison with them in that industrial city constituency, but in Dumfries, in which their local candidate had been in the field for many months before the by-election, they had finished only just ahead of us, and we had had a very short campaign with a candidate adopted at the very last minute.

I became convinced that we should either make a public pact with the Liberals based on a united front for self-government, or, by making an approach and being turned down, expose them as being fraudulent in their self-government claims. The first shot in my campaign was a letter to the *Scots Independent* in November 1963, in which I wrote, "Who can doubt the effectiveness of SNP propaganda in the winning of Liberal votes in Scotland?"

At National Council on 7th December 1963, I submitted a formal resolution asking Council to authorise an invitation to be issued in the name of the Party to the Scottish Liberal Party to arrange for a meeting between national office-bearers from each Party to negotiate a public pact, the details of which I spelled out. The motion was defeated.

National Council had a special meeting on 8th February 1964, to consider a massive reorganisation report which had been drawn up by Gordon Wilson, in consultation with the National Executive Committee. Towards the end of this meeting, when Tom Gibson, Editor of the *Scots Independent* and one of the pillars of the Party since 1928, had fortuitously left the chamber, the West Lothian delegates got approval from the meeting to have a resolution dealing with the Liberals on the agenda of the regular National Council meeting to be held on 7th March. Tom Gibson was totally opposed to what I had in mind as were several others.

By this time I was more familiar with how National Council operated and I made as much use as I could of my power base in West Lothian. Within the West Lothian Association, we had discussed the question of dealing with the Liberals at great length. We had called their bluff in West Lothian, at the by-election and in meetings which we had with them subsequently. We were convinced that they were of no real substance and that they traded mainly on the name of their once-great Party and on our propaganda for self-government. Even without organisation or members, they could always count on press coverage in a way which, at that time, the Scottish National Party could not.

By 7th March, I judged that the West Lothian resolution which had been lying on the table since 8th February, would not be passed by National Council because it went into too much detail, so West Lothian Constituency Association submitted a fresh resolution in the following terms: —

"As a preliminary to consideration of the West Lothian Constituency Association motion this council instructs that a letter be sent to the Scottish Liberal Party inviting their comment on the following: —

"1. Will the Scottish Liberal Party put self-government at the head of its electoral programme and make it a requirement that all its candidates pledge themselves to give priority to it in their campaigns?

"2. Will the Scottish Liberal Party and all its candidates pledge themselves jointly to demand Scottish self-government if and when a majority of Scottish seats are held by SNP or Liberal M.P.s, and to set up a Scottish Parliament if the Government of the day refuse to pass the necessary legislation?"

The debate in National Council was warm. The attacks on me and on my supporters, particularly those from West Lothian, and the doubts cast by speaker after speaker on our integrity and honesty infuriated me. As the mover of the resolution, it was my right to wind up the debate. I can remember throwing off my jacket and defending the resolution with all the passionate sincerity I could muster. To my surprise, and relief, the resolution was carried, authorising a letter to go to the Liberals, and the waiting press men were notified. West Lothian had previously publicised the fact that it was going to ask National Council to send this letter and various people, notably Michael Starforth, Treasurer of the Scottish Liberal Party, had written letters to the press expressing hopes that some sort of pact would be concluded.

The press communicated the result of the debate to the Chairman of the Scottish Liberal Party, John Bannerman. His public reply was the one which I had regretfully expected. It was not the one anticipated by those who hoped for a pact nor by those who feared that there might be a pact. It has stood us in good stead ever since because it exposed the totally opportunist attitude of the Liberal Party in Scotland towards the vital issue of self-government. When under pressure the Liberals admit, as John Bannerman did, that for them self-government ranks "in priority with defence, co-partnership, and other major Liberal policies."

His key remarks, as far as we were concerned, were: "Liberals supported the decentralisation of executive control from Westminster . . ." and "the Scottish Liberal Party, although autonomous, was part of the Great Britain Liberal Movement and would not contemplate any unilateral action for Scottish self-government. . . ." The Liberal road to travel was "self-government in our domestic affairs" and this aim ". . . can be realised through the Scottish, English and Welsh Liberal vote." John Bannerman made it absolutely clear that, in spite of their apparent autonomy, the Liberals were totally committed to the continued rule of Westminster even if the majority of the people of Scotland wanted self-government.

The reorganisation report from Gordon Wilson, to which I referred, was adopted by the Party early in 1964. Several constitutional changes were made which undoubtedly assisted the growth of the Party in the 1960s. At the time, Gordon Wilson was Assistant National Secretary, having been appointed to that post in 1963. One of the most important principles involved in his re-organisation was that of giving executive responsibility for particular spheres of activity to certain office-bearers, who were called Executive Vice-Chairmen. In 1964 there were two appointed—one for Organisation and the other for Publicity and Policy. The number was later increased to four.

In the period 1962 - 63, there was fairly intense activity going on in West Lothian. We were busy consolidating the progress we had made in 1962. New branches were formed, canvassing was carried out, meetings were held and the Party within the constituency had a general air of optimism. We were never particularly concerned to recruit a large number of members in West Lothian. Our attitude to membership subscriptions, which were fixed at a paltry level by National Council, was that their payment did not really make people active propagandists for self-government. Members who are really active often spend more in a week, in expenses, than the annual subscription. We were more concerned with recruitment of people who were prepared to work, rather than with building up a huge list of members who were mostly inactive.

At the first Annual General Meeting of West Lothian Constituency Association, in March 1963, Robert McIntyre was the guest speaker. He referred to an aspect of the Party's work which was a bone of contention then and which continues to bother some people today. After having referred to a recent Labour Party policy statement issued by a group of Scottish

Labour M.P.s in Glasgow as "incredibly and fantastically inadequate to meet the serious economic position in Scotland," he pointed out that "their supposed policy for Scotland is simply to carry on with ignoring Scotland's need to be treated as an economic and cultural unit and proposing such things as nationalisation and further centralisation in London to put the control of more and more Scots jobs in the hands of English majorities whose interests certainly do not reach as far as the Border."

Going on to deal with need for a Scottish Parliament, Dr McIntyre said, "The National Party's vigour in the past nine or twelve months has shown that it is moving fast to a point at which it will be able to say 'We can form a Government and here are the men and women who will form it.' It is the only Party which can revolutionise life in Scotland by having the sources of power for government in Scotland. It is revolutionary, socially as well as otherwise, because, with self-government in Scotland, we would inevitably create a new 'establishment' with an entirely different outlook from the present Tory/Labour/Liberal Unionist attitude."

Here, surely, in Robert McIntyre's vision, is one of the reasons for optimism about political life in Scotland after self-government has been achieved. Surely the people of Scotland want to be free for ever from the control of those who, for generations, have appeared to be Scottish, have spoken (some of them) with Scottish accents but who have been content merely with representing their constituencies in London, instead of *acting for Scotland* in relation to Scottish needs and aspirations. We will want realists who will *act* for Scotland. These minions of the English Parties who have represented Scotland in London will have to do some radical re-thinking if they are to bid for responsibility in a free Scotland.

As the Scottish National Party gains the confidence of the people of Scotland, the Labour Unionists, the Tory Unionists, the Liberal Unionists will all lose power—and they are unlikely to recover it. New political institutions will arise in Scotland and a new orientation will take place.

The holding of power is a sacred trust and one does not need to look to history to see that those who have power like to hold on to it. One need only look at the present situation with regard to political broadcasting in Scotland, in which the Scottish National Party is restricted to five minutes per year while the Liberals, who got fewer votes at the last General Election— 147,667 as against the SNP vote of 306,854—get at least four

41

times as much. Not that the Liberals have any power, but as they are totally ineffective in U.K. terms, the real power holders, the Tory and Labour Parties, can afford to try and look democratic by allowing the Liberals quite disproportionate amounts of time for Party Political Broadcasting, knowing that they are no real threat to them or to their power bases.

When the people of Scotland give power to the Scottish National Party they must be confident of at least two things—the ability of the Scottish National Party leadership, particularly its Parliamentary candidates, to form a provisional Government capable of being responsible to the people of Scotland in an effective way and, secondly, the people must have confidence in the Party's integrity in relation to its attitude of democracy. In other words we must continue to give a guarantee, as the Party has always guaranteed, that when the people of Scotland vote for independence by voting for the SNP they know that a thoroughly democratic constitution will be submitted to the people and that a General Election will be held immediately thereafter.

It is all very well to repeat these things, but people must be convinced of our belief in them and in our ability to stick to them. To evoke such conviction requires in us a strength which only the maturity of experience brings. That is one of the reasons why the constitutional way to self-government is a long road and a hard road to travel.

The people of Scotland do not change their voting loyalties lightly. That has been proved in generations of election results. Most people, before they will change their vote, have to be convinced. This is quite clear from the fact that although seventy-five per cent or more of the people of Scotland want self-government in some form or another, many of them require to be convinced of two things— one, that Scotland is capable of running its own affairs and two, that the Scottish National Party is responsible enough and effective enough to be trusted with votes to enable it to secure self-government.

Robert McIntyre and Arthur Donaldson have both ploughed the self-government furrow longer than I have. They received sufficient encouragement in the early 1940s to believe that the SNP would eventually win the support of the majority of the people of Scotland. That encouragement carried them through the late 1940s and the 1950s. When Robert McIntyre spoke in Linlithgow in March 1963, he had completed a twenty-five-year stent and he believed that he saw real progress towards the evolution of a new Scottish "establishment." I have no doubt that he was right.

In contrast, a few weeks later, I attended a one-day conference sponsored by the Town and Country Planning Association (Scottish section). The subject was "The Scottish Economy Today" and in a report to the Party, having attended as a delegate from the SNP, I described the Conference as "a musty airing cupboard for out-of-date and ineffective United Kingdom misconceptions about, and ineffective planning for, Scotland, which must have disappointed the bulk of the people who troubled to attend." The morning session was taken by the Board of Trade Controller for Scotland and the afternoon session was taken by Mr J. N. Toothill, the Managing Director of Ferranti's in Scotland.

Getting an opportunity to speak, I deplored the lack of urgency in the speeches made at the conference and reminded those present that they were dealing with men's lives, that there were over one hundred thousand people in Scotland unemployed and that it was deplorable that nothing really effective was being done for them by the English government. I took exception to the constant talk of bringing in people and skills to Scotland, saying, "I believe that this paternalist and patronising attitude will never be as successful as would be the same amount of effort spent on giving the Scottish people opportunities for their own enterprise and capital to be used in giving their fellow Scots employment." I still believe that, more emphatically than ever. The inference that the Scots cannot run their own economy is typical of the insidious propaganda which the English parties have spread around Scotland for years, undermining the confidence of the Scots in themselves.

CHAPTER 4

A POLITICAL ACTIVIST, 1963-64

FOR MOST ACTIVE members of the SNP who attend, the
Party's Annual Conferences are enjoyable and interesting. All
branches fulfilling certain conditions are required to send delegates. They are also required to send in resolutions for the
agenda and nominations of persons to hold responsibility for a
year at a time at national level. In order to give branches
sufficient warning and to fulfil a timetable which enables amendments to be formally submitted before the agenda is printed,
the procedures take about five months. Like many other democratic arrangements they seem complicated to the uninitiated.
One of the results of the system is that although most branches
take part in the actual conference by sending delegates and
observers, a smaller number of branches takes part regularly in
the submission of resolutions and in the nomination of office-
bearers.

For the 1963 conference in Edinburgh a total of seventeen
branches featured in the agenda. A look at the list indicates
where the active strength of the SNP lay at that time—Aberdeen, Forfar, Perth, Dunfermline, Stirling, Dumbarton,
Greenock, Irvine Valley, Hamilton, Cambuslang, Uddingston,
Glasgow, Kirkintilloch, Bathgate, Whitburn, Blackburn, and
Westfield and Torphichen.

The state of affairs in 1963 may be compared with recent
conferences in which over one hundred branches have taken
part in submitting nominations and resolutions.

In 1963, out of eighty-eight nominations, eighty-one came
from only eight branches, all long-established. The younger
branches, such as those in West Lothian, did not contain people
who knew anything about the rest of the Party, so very few of
them made any nominations. Westfield and Torphichen Branch
was the only West Lothian Branch making a nomination, that of
myself for membership of National Council to which I had been
elected for the first time in the previous year. However, I had
also been nominated as a Vice-Chairman (the Party Constitution
allowed for two at that time), and this caused the only contest

44

for national office at that conference. I was elected and thus became the first "new boy" among the national office-bearers for several years.

Among other things, the 1963 Conference called on "The United Kingdom Government to cease the manufacturing, testing and stock-piling of all nuclear weapons," and it agreed that the voting age should be reduced to eighteen years. It dealt with the takeover by English concerns of Scottish firms and with the allocation of university places to Scottish students. The Conference asserted "that Treaties, International Agreements, etc., entered into by Great Britain or by the United Kingdom be not necessarily binding on the Scottish State." This resolution was one of fundamental importance for the future. It has been repeated subsequently on many occasions, and has been conveyed through diplomatic channels several times since 1963, to all the States of Europe, to the E.E.C. in Brussels, and to the United Nations Organisation.

Westfield and Torphichen Branch had two resolutions, neither of which was accepted by the Conference. One called on the SNP to take "immediate steps to form a Scottish Shadow Cabinet" and the other declared that "in the event of Scotland attaining self-government, all land in the country becomes the property of the State."

It has always been a disappointment to me, and, I am sure, to millions of others in the United Kingdom, that no London Government has yet taken effective steps to deal with the control of land use and land values. I have always believed that land belongs to the people and that those of us who have a title to "ownership" of land are really holding it in trust for the nation. Consequently, I am a strong supporter of control of development of land and of the introduction of a system whereby increases in the value of land benefit the national community, and not individuals. The escalation of property values in recent years, caused to a great extent by speculators, is clear evidence in favour of such a system.

We were fortunate to have in our branch John Dow, whose experience as an Inspector of Taxes and as a County Assessor for ten years contributed greatly to the several heated debates we had within the Branch, before we submitted the resolution and prepared the argument in support of it.

The arrangement we proposed was perfectly fair to people presently holding a title to land and, if implemented, would certainly be very much fairer to the community as a whole than the present system. What we proposed interfered in no way with individual or collective freedom to a greater extent than present United Kingdom legislation dealing with the control of use of land.

We proposed that present owner-occupiers would be given a lease of their ground and have as much security of tenure with their lease as they have at present holding title deeds. All owners of property and other occupiers of land would pay a site-rent to the state for the ground their buildings or agricultural works, etc., occupied. We suggested that the computation of values be carried out through the medium of the burgh and county valuation departments. Payment to owners could be made over a number of years by annuities, and there would be a right of appeal to a Board or Court in case of dispute between State and landowner over valuation. Payment would be based on the value of site at the time of takeover. If I ever take part in a Scottish Parliament I shall certainly favour legislation on these lines.

The other resolution which was lost was of lesser importance —the formation of a Scottish Shadow Cabinet. However, the time is not far off when Scotland will have a real Cabinet. As far as we in Scotland are concerned, there are already two Shadow Cabinets, both sitting in Westminster, almost indistinguishable from each other, in their chauvinist English outlook and in the disastrous effects their policies have had on Scotland. The day when their representatives in Scotland are rejected by the Scottish electorate will indeed be a happy one for the future of Scotland.

During the Conference, an Edinburgh University student gave me an idea which was to flourish in a way which was to satisfy the most optimistic hopes we could have held for it at that time. In 1963, the CND sign was to be seen everywhere. Randall Foggie, one of the members of the Edinburgh University Nationalist Club, urged on me the desirability of the Scottish National Party also having an instantly recognisable sign. After the Conference, on a train journey to England at the end of May, I worked on the idea and circulated a sketch to the office-bearers of West Lothian Constituency Association with the comment, "I am sure that somebody else could develop this idea and produce something more effective and a little simpler." That is precisely what happened.

What I produced was a combination of a St Andrew's Cross and a thistle. I gave my idea to an artist friend, William Millan, who taught Art in Bathgate, and he produced a series of variations. However, I was unable to make up my mind and on the recommendation of another friend, Frank Whitaker, the advertising and publicity manager of the Scottish Council (Development and Industry) I wrote to a young man of twenty, Julian Gibb, at that time employed by one of Scotland's leading commercial studios. He is undoubtedly a brilliant designer, and the SNP was very fortunate in having his help just when it proved to be most valuable. Working from the ideas which I gave him, he designed the symbol which was to become known throughout the whole of Scotland within five years as the emblem of the Party fighting for freedom and independence for Scotland. In fact, among William Millan's sketches there was one very like the symbol which Julian eventually designed. The production of the symbol was a joint effort and all those involved in it can take a share of the credit, but most of the credit must go to Julian Gibb, whose clarity of thought and expression, coupled with understanding of our aims as a Scottish political movement, evolved the final design. I then pushed on with the promotion of the symbol, using it in literature and in other ways.

At a meeting of West Lothian Constituency Association in August 1963, there were several interesting items on the agenda under the heading "Election Campaign." It was agreed that "an all-out fight should be made for Burgh and County Council seats in the 1964 elections." There was a suggestion that the Association produce a small cheap badge to be distributed free to children. I suggested that the SNP adopt a motif and proposed the combination referred to above. Angus McGillveray suggested that the Association print small sticky labels with the motif on them. A further suggestion was put forward that the Association produce car transfers. All these things were dealt with and an ambitious publicity and public relations programme for the constituency was launched.

West Lothian Association went ahead and decided to order at least 10,000 supporter badges, carrying the symbol in colour, for use in the forthcoming General Election campaign. The Association gave the National Executive Committee the opportunity of purchasing a further 15,000 but the offer was not taken up. Nevertheless, West Lothian ordered more than its own requirement and in fact, in the 1964 General Election, several other constituencies were enthusiastic about the symbol and bought badges from us.

Towards the end of 1963 we were going "flat out" in West Lothian in our preparations for the General Election campaign. I knew that, as prospective parliamentary candidate, I was not doing enough canvassing but I was so anxious that the Party produce certain publications in time for the Election, that I gave these responsibilities top priority. In a letter to Ian Macdonald on 30th December 1963, I said, "The leaflets on which I am working at present are as follows:

"1. A 'throw away' leaflet on the need for the SNP.

2. A sixteen-page 'popular' policy statement for people who are interested in the SNP.

3. A minimum of three election pamphlets.

4. As many policy documents as can be completed in time for the proposed conference on 14/15 February."

At that time the SNP was feverishly working several constituencies to be as well prepared as possible if Sir Alec Douglas Home chose March 1964 for the General Election.

Ian Macdonald must have been working about eighty hours a week. History will certainly record the value of his efforts in building up the organisation and strength of the Party throughout Scotland at this crucial period. Another person who was working very hard at this time at national level was Gordon Wilson, who was Assistant National Secretary. He had taken on the task of examining the Constitution and organisation of the Party in order to make it more effective politically, and was also concerned with maintaining the regular broadcasts in Edinburgh of Radio Free Scotland.

The subject of transport was prominent in the Scottish news at this time as the huge cuts in the railway system proposed by Dr Beeching, Chairman of British Railways Board, were taking effect. Opposition to the cuts had become organised in the North under the leadership of Mr Frank Thomson of Invergordon Distillers, with the support of many local people including that of Mr Phil Durham who became Secretary of the organisation. A North of Scotland "vigilantes" association was formed to campaign for the retention of certain vital services north of Inverness, and support flowed to the organisation from all over Scotland, often accompanied by pleas for the support of the association to combat threatened cuts in other parts of the country. This resulted in the association becoming "The Transport Conference of Scotland."

At this time, the Scottish National Party was not organised beyond Perth, apart from a nucleus of support in the Western Isles and an embryo organisation in the North-East centred on an active branch in Aberdeen and led by Bruce Cockie. The Party was expanding there, outwards from Aberdeen, and it was expanding fast in Fife, Clackmannanshire, Stirlingshire, the Lothians, the Borders and Dumfriesshire. It was also making encouraging growth in the Glasgow region. The hard core of competent activists were so involved on their own doorsteps that none had any time to go north to Inverness or beyond in order to try to capitalise on the transport situation there.

Many of the people in the north who were active in the Transport Conference of Scotland came to appreciate that only real political pressure would give any power to their protests. I am sure that many of them voted Liberal, as did many others who were similarly convinced without having taken part in the protest organisation. Many, in fact, were nationalists. The M.P. elected for Ross-shire, Alasdair Mackenzie, was entirely sympathetic to the idea of self-government as proposed by the SNP and admitted on several occasions that had it been a comparable SNP organisation which had asked him to stand for Parliament instead of a Liberal Party organisation, he could have accepted the nomination. However, although it was not present on the mainland of the Highlands at that time, the SNP existed in the Western Isles. Our leading activist of the time, Donald J. Stewart, the Provost of Stornoway and, in 1970, the first SNP Member of Parliament to be elected at a General Election, judged that (in 1964) the time was not yet ripe to contest.

The whole saga of the Scottish railways, from the centralisation of control in London in the 1920s to the Beeching cuts, the reactions of protest, the formation of the vigilantes, and their final total eclipse, teaches a lesson which the Scottish people seem unwilling to learn. The pattern of railway decline was similar to the results of Londonisation in the shale industry, the coal industry and many other industries which had fallen to English control. The common factor in the State-controlled industries was the almost total neglect, in ignorance, by English Governments, of the Scottish economic and industrial situation in the hungry 'twenties and 'thirties, through the second World War and right up to the 1960s. And that ignorance persists today, tempered only by the realisation of the great value of Scotland's oil resources.

Another smaller example of the same kind of thing was

49

happening with regard to Air Transport. During 1963, many people had become convinced that Prestwick should become Glasgow's airport. Under the auspices of SEISS I examined the history of civil aviation in Scotland and compiled a report which SEISS published.

The SNP made use of these statistics and drafted "Opportunity in the Air," a policy for civil aviation in Scotland, which was published in March 1964. It catalogued the shameful neglect of Prestwick Airport since it was founded in 1935—"one of the chief examples of opportunities lost by frustrating Government delay, broken Government promises and by consideration of London interests first and foremost. Such development as has taken place has been provided tardily and reluctantly." An abbreviated calendar in the policy statement catalogued the English attitude.

1944—The Air Ministry reported that "careful investigation shows that Prestwick will not provide even an aerodrome of local dimensions."

1945—The coalition Government was threatening to close Prestwick Airport and to transfer all the services to London. The opposition of Scots of all political loyalties (and the election of Dr Robert McIntyre as a Scottish National Party M.P.) saved the airport from the Government's axe. At this time the late Group-Captain D. F. McIntyre, D.F.C., of Scottish Aviation Limited, and many other individuals and bodies were already working hard envisaging a golden future for Prestwick Airport and for civil aviation in post-war Scotland.

1947—The Minister of Civil Aviation (in a Labour Government) said, "BEA will provide feeder services to Prestwick." (We are still waiting for these twenty-six years later.)

1949—The Labour Government threatened to reduce the services at Prestwick operated by the Scandinavian and Dutch air lines (SAS and KLM).

1953—"I can give your our pledge that all (Tory) Ministers are anxious that Prestwick shall advance"—Mr James Henderson Stewart, M.P., Tory Under-Secretary at the Scottish Office.

1953 - 1963—Continued pressure from Ayr County Council, the U.S.A. and airline companies had the runways extended and saw the eventual fulfilment of part of the development which should have taken place in the early 1950s at the latest.

1964—London decided to reduce the SAS international services at Prestwick, threatened to reduce KLM international services, and thus jeopardised Prestwick's whole future as an airport.

Then, in 1964, the Ministry of Civil Aviation, which had pursued the same anti-Scottish policies without variation, irrespective of whether the Government was Tory or Labour, successfully played off Edinburgh interest against Glasgow interest by encouraging Glasgow Corporation to have a new airport at Abbotsinch. I am convinced that if Scottish interests had co-operated under the leadership of Ayr County Council in early 1963, Prestwick would have been developed as Glasgow's first airport in time to take over the domestic services which were then being operated at Renfrew Airport which was due for closure because it had no room to expand.

Encouraged by the people I had met in Prestwick and in Ayr when drafting the Civil Aviation Policy, notably David Reid, Secretary of Prestwick Development Association, and Tom Henderson, a young SNP activist in Prestwick, and also encouraged by the success of Frank Thomson and his railway vigilantes, the SNP stirred the people of Prestwick into launching the "Civil Aviation Development Association for Scotland" with the by-name of "Scotjet." The initial meeting was arranged by the SNP although it was made perfectly clear by the Chairman of the meeting, Provost Ian Foulds of Prestwick, that the new "Vigilantes of the Air" would not be an organ of the SNP and that members of all political parties would be welcome in "Scotjet."

Over three hundred people attended the launching meeting and the Association got off to an enthusiastic start. The aims of the Association were to publicise the advantages of Prestwick Airport and to campaign for full development of its potential as an international airport; and to co-operate with all persons, local authorities and other bodies throughout Scotland and elsewhere who were interested in promoting the expansion of civil aviation in general and Prestwick Airport services in particular.

However, we were about a year too late to have any real hope of achieving anything. Another reason, which may seem extraordinary to some, is the fact that SNP sponsorship made the organisation untouchable in the eyes of the Tory and Labour Parties, particularly the latter. It must be perfectly clear to any spectator that of all the political parties, the Scottish National Party is primarily concerned with the good of Scotland and the welfare of the Scottish people, but ignorance, jealousy and professional political rivalry, seem to exert more influence on the leaders of the Tory and Labour Parties in Scotland than the pressure of the needs of the people, especially when the latter are expressed by spokesmen of the Scottish National Party. A factor is, of course, that the National Party contests against these parties, seeking the votes of the electorate.

"Scotjet" went the way of other similar organisations but before it disappeared, it produced a very sensible plan for making Prestwick into Glasgow's international airport. It proposed that St Enoch Station in Glasgow should become Glasgow's central air terminal with a regular fast rail service via Paisley to the airport railway station. Provision for this had already been included in the Prestwick plans. This would have enabled the centre of Glasgow to be linked to Prestwick with a train service taking only about thirty minutes, including a stop at Paisley. The provision of motorway from Prestwick to Glasgow would have enabled motorists to do the trip in not much more.

It all seemed so sensible, making full use of our existing valuable resources, and it would have produced a really profitable airport at Prestwick. The trouble was that such a plan would have resulted in Prestwick attracting international traffic, both outward and inward, away from London. Prestwick is a Scottish resource. It clearly had great potential value in assisting the development of Scotland, in international commerce and trade as well as in tourist traffic, but no matter how many people in Scotland wanted it to be developed, it could not be developed because a political decision was necessary and the Scots did not have the political power to do anything about it. London government had the power and English interests came first. Has it ever been any different since James VI took the Scottish Court to London in 1603?

Another matter reflecting the impotence of the people of Scotland was going on at the same time. At a SEISS meeting in Edinburgh in March 1964, Professor Ritchie Calder revealed the selfish "narrow nationalism" of the English Government, in its attitude to the proposed new World Health Centre. The representatives of the other nations in the world were apparently in favour of the new centre being established in Scotland, a country long famed for medical research, yet the British (English?) attitude was to oppose establishing a World Health Centre in Scotland on the grounds that Britain might lose her top medical scientists to the work of the Centre. Can anyone doubt that an independent Scottish Parliament would have taken a different attitude? Would Westminster have opposed the World Health Organisation if they had chosen Oxford or Cambridge?

As summer came, it became clear that Parliament would not be dissolved until the autumn, and the activists of the SNP breathed sighs of relief because they believed that the more time they got for their campaign, the more votes they would win. At this stage it looked as if we would fight ten or twelve seats—the largest number ever before having been eight. In West Lothian we started campaigning in real earnest in July, accompanied by a newspaper advertising campaign which ran on until the General Election in October. Nyasaland (now known as Malawi) had just been granted independence, so our first advertisement read: "Nyasaland now has independence—what about Scotland—but of course Scotland is a profitable colony. So long as we are a nation of labourers in our own land we will remain England's last satellite."

Our weekly advertisements dealt with many other topical subjects. The visit of the EFTA Council to Edinburgh gave us an opportunity to compare Scotland with Norway and other countries in the European Free Trade Association.

We pointed out that in the previous twelve years the number of jobs for men in Scotland had gone down by forty thousand, while in the same period the number of jobs for men South of the Border had increased by nearly nine hundred thousand. We referred to the net emigration of more than three hundred thousand Scots in the previous twelve years—a figure equal to the total number of men working in the cities of Glasgow and Aberdeen added together. We pointed out that Scotland, with twenty-four per cent of the mileage of Class I trunk roads in the United Kingdom had only fourteen per cent of the U.K. spending on such roads. And so on—facts and comparisons were our political ammunition and we kept on using them.

In August 1964, the Party held a two-day convention for candidates and election agents in the village of Torphichen. In the course of it, the Chairman, Arthur Donaldson, announced

53

that we would contest fifteen seats. We were not allowed to take part in Party Political Broadcasting at this time because the current U.K. rules stated that a party must contest fifty seats. This was clearly totally unjust in the case of Scotland and not only unjust but ridiculous in the case of Wales. Scotland had seventy-one constituencies and Wales thirty-six. However, this was typical and continues to be typical of the way in which the English parties make the rules to suit themselves and to keep the Scottish National Party and Plaid Cymru (the Welsh Nationalist Party) off the air. In his press conference in Torphichen, Arthur Donaldson pointed out that if fifty was an appropriate figure for the United Kingdom, then the equivalent figure for Scotland would be six.

However, realising that they would have to appear democratic and give some token recognition of our existence, the English parties and the Broadcasting authorities agreed that any party fighting twenty per cent of the seats in Scotland could have participation in the election discussion programmes, even if they were not allowed time for Party Political Broadcasts. That is why we had fifteen candidates. In fact we had experienced some difficulty in getting a fifteenth constituency to fight, because of insufficient funds and organisation. The fifteenth constituency was that of Roxburgh, Selkirk and Peebles. The candidate was Anthony J. C. Kerr, a brilliant and unusual man who turned out to be quite uncontrollable. He was expelled from the Party in 1965 when he stood as an Independent candidate in the Borders by-election in defiance of a Party decision, both local and national, not to contest. He was readmitted in 1973.

We had a tremendous campaign in West Lothian. I had given up my job at the end of March 1964 in order to work full-time on political effort. We thought we could possibly win West Lothian if we worked hard enough. I was criticised in the constituency for not doing enough local work and for spending too much time on national affairs. In fact, a room of the new home into which we moved in Torphichen in August became the publicity nerve centre of the Party, while Ian Macdonald at Headquarters in Glasgow ran the organisational nerve centre. I certainly spent a considerable amount of time on SNP matters not directly affecting West Lothian.

We produced some very good leaflets in our 1964 contest, many of which were compiled by Willie Kellock. We used the symbol for the first time on posters and stickers of all sizes and on our lapel badges. We saved the latter until the actual election campaign when, of course, they were tremendously popular. Thousands of adults and children wore them.

As usual, the Tories had a new candidate, as did the Communists. The Liberals did not appear. The Tories had engaged a full-time Agent earlier in the year who quite sensibly concentrated her work on ensuring the saving of the deposit to avoid another red Tory face.

In the spring I had completed the drafting of *SNP and You* and had submitted it to National Council and then, having noted National Council's comments, to Annual Conference. Julian Gibb had gone through it with me word by word and had produced an excellent design for its format, and it was ready in time for the General Election. Its press coverage on release was very encouraging and it was eagerly distributed by the Party throughout the campaign. In fact, it eventually ran to three editions, being updated each time, and it was still the Party's main policy document in the 1970 Election. Over half-a-million copies of it have been sold.

SNP and You was the policy document which I had envisaged after the 1962 by-election. Its contents were drawn from the speeches, writings and comments of a great many people, as well as from the policies the Party had evolved in conference. It was both policy and propaganda and, more important, it aimed to draw together the ideals and the current philosophical outlook of a new political force in Scotland. It contained a clear statement of the democratic principles which the SNP wanted to see implemented in a free Scotland.

It aimed, without arrogance, to convey a proper sense of confidence and self-respect to the people of Scotland—not satisfaction with the state of Scotland; in fact, quite the reverse. I believed that, above all, the Scottish people needed to find confidence in themselves. The introduction summed it up.

"People ask why they should support the National Party. The National Party stands for the nation; all sections, all people in it; welded in a common purpose; devoted, dedicated to the social and economic improvement of all. The SNP stands for pride in a courageous and adult Scotland, and for confidence in a future guided by *your hands* and by the hands of your children. Our slogan is "PUT SCOTLAND FIRST"—a slogan of which we are proud—a slogan which no other politicians can use because the National Party is the only Scottish Political Party."

The pamphlet went on to answer the question, "Why Put Scotland First?"

"We want prosperity for our nation. We want bread for our people. But we want dignity too. For we know that bread is not enough to sustain the lives of men. We want health for our cities. But we want more than that—graciousness and breadth and beauty too.

"We turn envious eyes upon the spacious cities of the little lands which ought, by all the arguments of the Westminster politicians, to be poor and wretched. We think of Stockholm and Copenhagen, Oslo and Amsterdam, and then compare Glasgow and Edinburgh and other places with wretched slums: and we look south to England where wages are so much higher and wealth so much more plentiful, at our expense, for there is no doubt that we subsidise England, under Unionist rule—Tory or Labour or Liberal; and that we help to keep London and Birmingham rich and help to keep unemployment there down to a quarter of the Scottish rate.

"Those are two of the reasons why the SNP looks for your support, and your loyalties."

There followed a section on "Facts," highlighting the needs of Scotland and on the inadequate action taken by successive Governments. It referred to the "whip-hand discretion against Scotland which amounted, in direct taxation alone, to at least another £1250 million in the last ten years. This is the amount, based on Government figures and conservative estimates, which you have paid to London and which was neither spent in Scotland, nor for the benefit of Scotland." The earlier financial drain mentioned was the cost of educating emigrants, "but the main cost (of emigration) to Scotland is the loss to our present and our future of all these hearts and brains, these muscles and minds, which should have been contributing to the happiness and prosperity of the land which bore them."

The next section was the one with the most fundamental importance—"What the SNP Democrats seek—our golden visions—and our faith. What we seek for Scotland is plain— freedom through unity—freedom and power to rule herself, reform herself, respect herself.

"There is only one road on which to seek this power, this freedom. That is the political road; the road of democratic support for a party with high ideals, unselfish aims and practical policies.

"The SNP believes that all human beings, no matter how different in gift and achievement, are entitled to equal opportunity and consideration and that society should be developed and wealth distributed so as to give everyone the freedom and dignity which is their right.

"The SNP recognises the need to build towards a true fraternity of all nations.

"SNP Policy is based on the rule of law; freedom of conscience, expression and worship; collective defence and positive measures to remove the poverty and injustice which threaten the peace of the world.

"An SNP Democrat believes in the progressive development of national and local government, and other institutions, towards the greatest possible diffusion of democratic powers.

"An SNP Democrat recognises that happiness and dignity depend not only on possessions, but on things in which people are able to take a lively and deep interest beyond their own private lives.

"To an SNP Democrat, sound and practical policies are those which will ensure that all are decently housed and in good health, and that all have an equal chance of living active and happy lives, and of developing the talent with which they are endowed.

"An SNP Democrat's patriotism is expressed in pride in his country's achievements, by recognition of its place among the nations and its duties to mankind, in the desire to regenerate the Scottish people and plan boldly for their country—seeking for Scotland nothing less than the best.

"The SNP will achieve these aims through the democratic support of the Scottish people at the polls. We are a nation. We must act as one so that the rest of the world sees clearly that the Scottish people mean to accept the responsibilities of an adult twentieth-century nation."

These aims and ideals were then extended into practical policies dealing with employment, finance, agriculture, forestry, fishing, housing, education, sport, recreation, the arts, social services and defence. A final section in the booklet dealt with "The Lies" which at that time were commonly used in anti-SNP propaganda, e.g. that "The Scots have always wanted to roam, wanted to emigrate and wanted adventure abroad," and that "The Scots always do better out of Scotland as there are so few opportunities here," and, of course, the hardy old chestnut which is even further from the truth now in 1973 than ever before that "Scotland is a poor country subsidised by England and unable to support herself."

The last section was entitled "Your Help." It briefly outlined the recent history of the SNP and stressed that "the supreme need of Scotland is the re-establishment of a Scottish Parliament."

That was the theme of our Election Campaign in 1964. We had a great cause, we had good propaganda material, attractive in design and carefully worded in content. We had a good and enthusiastic team throughout West Lothian. In May, we had scored our first success in County Council and District Council Elections when John Hamilton had been elected to the County Council and Robert Kerr to the District Council, both for the Westfield and Torphichen division. We had contested a number of seats and had done reasonably well throughout the country, considering it was our first attack on any scale on what had been an undisputed Labour stronghold for nearly 20 years.

The result in West Lothian in the 1964 General Election totally confirmed my dedication to the cause of self-government for Scotland. The 1962 by-election result had been dismissed by opponents and by some commentators as an aberration, a flash in the pan, and in other familiar phrases. Even the most sympathetic journalists, and there were a few, who visited West Lothian during the 1964 General Election campaign were highly sceptical, for perfectly sound reasons, of our estimate, first calculated about a month before polling day, that we would score 15,000 votes. In the event, we had 89 votes to spare. We splashed an advertisement in each of the local papers saying "Thanks—Thanks—Thanks—On behalf of the younger generation to whom the future of Scotland is most important, the SNP expresses thanks to the 15,089 voters who voted for Billy Wolfe last Thursday." We promised that "The work of the SNP will go on with renewed vigour after this great show of confidence—an increase of nearly 5500 votes."

The morale of the Party in West Lothian was certainly high. The West Lothian team had been led by an outstanding and most attractive person—Vera Maclay—a student at Edinburgh University who was only 21 that year. I can remember an occasion in our Election rooms in Bathgate during the campaign when a well-known journalist, having had to wait till I could see him, thought he would brighten his day by dallying with the beautiful girl who was so busy at her desk. He got a straight answer, and when I told him later that the young lady was the Chairman of the Constituency Association, he had a new-found respect for the SNP in West Lothian. My Election Agent was Jimmy McGinley, a very able and direct person who had joined us at the end of the by-election campaign two years earlier. He had already been an active community worker in several organisations and his experience and knowledge were very useful to us.

Vera Maclay and Jimmy McGinley were exceptionally good as Chairman and Election Agent respectively. They were key members in a strong team representative of many parts of the County. The stalwarts of 1962 and earlier were still to the fore, Willie Kellock and Charlie Auld in Bo'ness, John Hamilton and Danny McDonald in Westfield, Robert Kerr and Iain Arbuckle in Torphichen and Angus McGillveray in East Whitburn. By this time, Angus had become involved in fund-raising for the Party nationally, having started a weekly sweep ticket called Alba Pools. He was also building up the Publications Department as honorary manager. It had been started with donations from a handful of people who contributed altogether not much more than £200. Within five or six years, the value of the fund was well into four figures, such was the growth of the Party and the increase in output of leaflets, posters, badges, etc.

Among the newer members, Willie Hardie in South Queensferry and Alex Sibbald in Whitburn did a tremendous amount of work for weeks prior to the 1964 Election. Many members took their summer holidays to work in the campaign and, for weeks when they were not on holiday, many of them turned out night after night canvassing, bill-posting and preparing the electoral organisation for Polling Day.

When the day of the contest arrived, we were probably prepared as well as, if not better than, any other SNP organisation had ever been.. We were certainly better prepared than we had been in 1962. Nevertheless, we knew that our organisation did not match up to that of the Labour Party.

The West Lothian campaign and keeping in close touch with the fourteen others candidates in the two or three months prior to polling day taught me a lot about politics and about electioneering—two quite separate and different subjects. I learned that although a party's aim may be capable of simple expression, as is the aim of the Scottish National Party, the work in trying to achieve the aim is exceedingly complex, depending as it does for success on influencing the hearts and the minds of tens of thousands of individual people in each constituency towards a major change in the way of life of a nation.

Having foreseen that I would want to work full time as long as possible in the forthcoming General Election campaign, I had decided in 1963 that I would give up my job the following spring.

I knew that I would require a job which permitted me to take time off irregularly and sometimes substantially, so at the end of 1964 I became Managing Director of an old spade forge in Plains, near Airdrie, which specialised in tools for forestry. After moving to Bathgate and incorporating the remnant of another similar company, the enterprise was renamed Chieftain Forge Ltd. We set out to give the forestry industry in the British Isles a complete service in tools and machinery.

My choice of an independent course in material terms so that I could have an independent course in political terms has meant that my family life has suffered. Our happy family circle in all these years in which my chair has very often been empty is a testimony to the love and unselfishness of my wife.

CHAPTER 5

THE PRESSURE BUILDS UP, 1964-65

THE TOTAL SNP vote in the 1964 General Election was 64,053. The most significant result was in West Lothian, as it proved what could be done to improve on a good by-election result. How had we in West Lothian been so successful in increasing the SNP vote? Simply by hard work intelligently directed and carried out by dedicated people, who were inspired with confidence in a future which was dependent on their efforts. Oliver Brown, writing to me a few weeks later, called it "the only ray of hope in what seems a dismal situation." It certainly gave great encouragement to the Party throughout Scotland and the galloping recruitment campaign continued.

Our campaign in West Lothian and its overall result had two particular aspects I would like to mention. The first was organisational or, to be more exact, financial. We had financed both the by-election campaign of 1962 and the General Election campaign two years later almost entirely ourselves at a total cost of about £3,500, including expenditure outside the actual statutory election periods. In November 1964, we were in the red to the tune of three or four hundred pounds. We continued to run on an overdraft or on loans for about six years thereafter. In West Lothian, we believed that it was essential to have money and to spend it on campaigns, but in common with the rest of the Party we had no regular source of revenue apart from our weekly pools tickets which a few members sold faithfully each week.

The other aspect which is worthy of mention is the effect on the Labour Party in West Lothian. Quite clearly they retained the seat comfortably but, also quite clearly, the SNP became their Enemy No. 1. The Labour Party's reaction to the SNP in West Lothian from 1964 onwards was an accurate sample reflection of the Labour Party's reaction to the SNP throughout Scotland from 1968 onwards, especially where the SNP campaign was strong.

Our main local opponent, Mr Tam Dalyell, the sitting Labour M.P., was an able representative of his constituency, very active and particularly well aware of the need to keep the electorate informed of what he was doing. Quite naturally, we had at

61

various times crossed swords in the local press, etc. Mr Dalyell had been particularly critical of my repeated claim that far from England subsidising Scotland, the reverse was the case. It is not surprising that he reacted on this subject because I had illustrated my arguments for self-government both in 1962 and especially in 1964 with relevant facts and figures, and these arguments won support. In fact, my Election Address in 1964 was mainly a draft Scottish Budget prepared with great care after much study and research.

The figures have not much more than a historic interest now, mainly because of the irrefutable fact that Scottish oil wealth makes it quite clear that as the oil flows, Scotland will subsidise England very substantially, unless she gains control of her own affairs through self-government. However, in 1964 the subject of London governments' taxation of, and spending in and for, Scotland was a hot one and on more than one occasion I had issued challenges to Mr Dalyell to debate the subject with me. The challenge was renewed at the end of 1964 and again in early 1965 but the debate did not actually take place until early 1966 in reaction to a repeat of the challenge, this time from the SNP in Glasgow. As Government spokesmen and apologists can always invoke the authority of the Treasury for their figures and as no figures were published for some very important areas of revenue and expenditure on Government account, this debate was inconclusive except for those who went to the debate with their minds made up beforehand. Prejudices were confirmed and the audience members were more interested in the performance of the speakers than in checking the arithmetic.

The person who first advanced a really detailed argument and who set out all the figures clearly and showed a subsidy from Scotland to England was Mr James Porteous. This was one of the results of the Covenant Campaign of the late '40s and early '50s, because in response and in reaction the Government published a White Paper, *Revenue and Expenditure (England and Wales and Scotland) 1952 - 53.* It purported to show that Scotland received more than the share she contributed to the United Kingdom Treasury in taxation. However, Mr Porteous, a former Secretary of what is now the Scottish Council (Development and Industry), and an economist well versed in the complexities of Government finance and with a special knowledge of the economic situation in Scotland, published a report on a detailed examination of the White Paper.

It was a scholarly production and Mr Porteous showed quite

clearly and conclusively that the White Paper presented a very biased picture of expenditure figures. His well reasoned conclusions show that over £88 million in 1952 - 53 (21·65% of Scottish revenue) was the net outflow of money from Scotland on Government account. He said in his report, "This is a staggering figure for a country the size of Scotland but it may be compared with the estimate made by the Political Economy Department of Glasgow University for 1946 - 47 and for 1947 - 48 of the net outflow of taxation from Scotland after deducting all Government payments in Scotland. This estimate was an average of between £55½ millions and £108 millions."

The work done by Mr Porteous and the conclusions which he published have never been seriously challenged. They have been ridiculed but they have never been challenged.

In 1964 the SNP Economics Committee carried out a very careful and objective examination on the lines of Mr Porteous' earlier work and with his active help. For 1964 - 65 we estimated a subsidy to England of £143 million. I have not the slightest doubt that it was a reasonably accurate estimate.

The area in which the largest discrepancies were found was in defence expenditure. To Anglo-Scots and to those who may call themselves Scottish second and British first, the fact that the contribution from Scotland towards defence is not necessarily spent on or in Scotland seems to be of little consequence, but to a Scot with my kind of outlook it is only reasonable that an equivalent amount of our taxation should be spent on or in Scotland to recirculate within our economy the wealth which we have created and earned here.

My main reason for using such figures was to endeavour to kill the myths circulated by our Tory and Labour opponents that Scotland is such a poor country that she couldn't possibly afford self-government. It is a poor reflection on the independent spirit of the Scots that such a querulous argument, based as it is on fear and greed, should have gained any currency. It is also a reflection on the loyalty of those who used the argument. What do such people say to the people of countries like Bangladesh and Vietnam, where freedom is not measured in terms of imperialist money?

There was tremendous pressure on the Party's Economics Committee at this time to deal with many matters other than the "Scottish Taxation Account" and the "Draft Scottish Budget" which had both been produced in time for the 1964 General Election. I reported to the December 1964 meeting of

National Council that "the most urgent need in policy matters appeared to be in local government, education, housing, transport, fuel and industrial development. Rating and taxation and legal reform are subjects which should also be dealt with as soon as possible but the first-named list is of greater importance from the short-term point of view. The formation of a committee to advise on the establishment of an Academy of the Arts is in hand."

It is important to involve members of an organisation in participating as much as possible. The SNP did just that in every field of political work at this period in its growth. We held an economic conference in April 1965, aiming to have three particular groups of people well represented—economists, statisticians and other experts able to give the Party a professional viewpoint of specific economic matters of importance to Scotland; prospective candidates for local government and for parliament and other persons likely to be speakers for the SNP; and active SNP members who were in close touch with the electorate, with a good idea of what voters are interested in.

We dealt with four subjects—the first was steel, on which the speaker was David Murray, writer on industrial and economic affairs. He also dealt with fuel and power. David Roxburgh, Strathclyde University's Industrial Liaison Officer, spoke on scientific industrial development and we had a symposium on land use and development. It was probably the most important subject dealt with at the conference and it laid the foundations for policies dealing with land use in general and with agriculture and forestry in particular. The speakers were Dr R. M. Gorrie, Editor of *Scottish Forestry*; James Johnston, a former President of the National Farmers' Union of Scotland; and A. A. Munro, the Head Forester of Novar Estates in Ross-shire. The chairman was a hill-farming research scientist, Andrew Currie.

In this period (1965) the Party produced some very useful documents on subjects such as local government, including proposals for local government reform, a national health service for Scotland, and a defence policy with special reference to the nuclear complex at the Holy Loch and Faslane.

These are examples of some of the things the Party was doing. We made use of every contact we had whether they were known supporters of the Party or not. We worked on the basis that they could only say no—and many did, or did not reply.

A related activity was the organisation of research with the object of producing propaganda and developing policy. We were still nowhere near the position of being able to employ a professional research officer. In fact, in my report to the 1965 Annual Conference, I made a plea for an allocation of sufficient money simply to buy Government and other publications to provide a library for the use of the volunteer research workers we had, who at that time were led by Alan Erasmusson, a brilliant young scientist not long out of University.

At this time, the Party had two Executive Vice-Chairmen— one dealing with "Publicity and Development" and the other dealing with "Organisation and Finance." My responsibilities were the former ones, the latter being held by Douglas Drysdale, who had been the Party's candidate in East Stirlingshire and Clackmannanshire in the 1964 election. He gave a tremendous amount of time and energy to the Party at this period and played an important part in the general direction of the Party's thought as well as in organisational and financial matters. He was Chairman and Managing Director of a foundry and engineering business in Larbert and as, at that time, he had no right-hand man on whom he could place complete reliance, he worked under a tremendous strain and it was not a great surprise that his health gave way a year or two later and he had to give up Party activity.

The Social and Economic Inquiry Society of Scotland, of which I was then Chairman, was also very active at this period and one of our main efforts in 1965 was to hold a conference on transport in Scotland at which the principal guest speaker was Professor E. R. Hondelink, the United Nations and World Bank Transport Consultant. The proceedings of that conference made a valuable contribution to discussion of the subject and provided a great deal of useful material for policy work and research. The Transport Conference was well supported by the remnants of the North of Scotland Vigilantes' Association although it dealt fully with all forms of transport and not just rail transport.

The need to have some sort of publicity organisation had been apparent for a considerable time and, early in 1965, Rosemary Hall, a first-class organiser and administrator, became honorary Publicity Secretary, though she had no professional training in such work. In the year in which she held this appointment, before becoming Organising Secretary of the Party in 1966, she issued over one hundred press releases, a much higher output than previous years. She very often spent ten to twelve hours a day in the SNP office in Edinburgh, carrying out all the secretarial and administrative work in connection with policy, organisation of conferences, most of the SEISSS work and all the general publicity.

As the Party grew, its demand for publicity grew and was never satisfied. In 1965, we had great difficulty in coping with the tide of events which was undoubtedly running in our favour. In my report to the Annual Conference that year I said, "The current development of the Party is almost a natural process in that conditions favour it at the present time and it takes place almost without effort by any existing part of our organisation." As far as planned development was concerned, with the limited resources of money and manpower and time which we had, I suggested that it must be looked on in the same way as a commander looks at a situation in warfare, to make progress with the minimal cost in lives and materials.

I suggested that there were three stages in the change in the climate of opinion which opposed our struggle: 1, Ridicule; 2, Toleration and friendly banter; and 3, Gloves off, savage and dirty. I said that if we spread our limited resources too thinly on the widest possible front, we would never get beyond stage 2. "Only by concentrating on bridge-heads where we can see the people really accepting us and turning our way can we win and hold positions of real power." A look through speeches, press statements, correspondence and minutes for this period shows how involved the Party was becoming in everyday political situations in Scotland, in efforts to win such power.

In June 1965, National Council debated a resolution which, to my knowledge, provided the first opportunity for the Party formally to discuss religious segregation in Scottish schools. It had been debated throughout West Lothian and had the support of all the West Lothian Branches. The resolution, which was defeated 31 to 17, was as follows:

"Noting a lessening in tension of the various denominations of the Christian Church in Scotland, the Scottish National Party urges its extension to the schools so that there may be an end to segregation at school age. Recognising the rights of parents, however, to safeguard the atmosphere in which their children shall be educated, this Party calls upon the Scottish Education Department to take the initiative in opening discussions with various churches in order that an agreed solution may be achieved."

To many, this is a very vexed question and it certainly inflames feelings, but I have little doubt that the segregated school system results in our having a divided society in our communities and in the nation in ways which depreciate our humanity.

I can quite understand the R.C. Church seeking and requiring the privileges it has in Scotland in a context of anti-R.C. discrimination encouraged by government and by the law; but in a free and democratic society in the laws of which no such discrimination exists, I believe that the continued segregation actually breeds discrimination by perpetuating a kind of second-class citizenship, echoing an earlier and less tolerant and less egalitarian age.

The subject has been discussed since 1965 on more than one occasion in the Party and the principles of the foregoing resolution are now accepted as part of our educational policy.

In industrial matters, the Party had founded an Association of Scottish Nationalist Trade Unionists with a view to gaining acceptance in Trade Union circles for the Party's aim of self-government for Scotland. In my own home constituency of West Lothian, there was plenty of trouble at that time in B.M.C. and in August 1965, I made reference to it when I was re-adopted as prospective candidate. I said that when B.M.C. had come to Scotland, it had been given a first-class opportunity to develop real confidence in Scotland but this had been thrown away and in its place were insecurity, superiority, restrictions and mistrust. "The men working the B.M.C. factory are frustrated," I said, "and this in an undertaking where co-operation should be the keynote." Among the grievances I listed were—lack of a production bonus incentive, class distinction barriers and multitudinous rules and regulations.

"All these," I said, "are rightly resented," and I laid the main responsibility for remedying the discords at the door of management. "There are troubles on both sides and there are men of sincerity and goodwill on both sides, but it is from the top that the initiative must come to break the attitude of violence encircling the factory like a black cloud."

In fact, within a year the top management was changed and industrial relations were much improved for two or three years at least.

In West Lothian, we also came out against "interference in the affairs of Vietnam by any power. Scotland knows only too well what interference in her own affairs means and should not support it in the case of other nations." The occasion for this statement was the action by U.S.A. in rushing another 50,000 men to the Vietnam theatre of war. There was a momentary world war scare and we pointed out to the people of West Lothian that the U.S. and U.K. Polaris bases in Scotland placed us in more imminent danger of a reprisal attack than the rest of the United Kingdom. I gave my support to a "Peace in Vietnam" group centred in Falkirk.

Later in the year, the SNP tackled the Labour Prime Minister, Mr Harold Wilson, over developments of a British Polaris base in the Gareloch. In reply, the Prime Minister said that "because of large sums being spent on fitting out the Gareloch base, there could be no question at this stage of moving it to some other place. Operational factors," said the Prime Minister, "were the governing factors in the selection of the base." Our comment was: "It's only votes in Scotland that Harold Wilson is interested in. He is not interested in the voters."

At our Conference that year, we passed a resolution from Paisley Branch: "In the belief that hereditary life titles are superfluous in modern democratic society, this Conference of the Scottish National Party calls for the abolition of these titles." The Party also gave its approval to "the single transferable vote system which has contributed directly to democracy and progress in Europe."

Internally, the Party's Publications Department flourished at this time, with the publication of many leaflets and pamphlets. A Scottish silversmith was commissioned through the Scottish Craft Centre to design a brooch based on the SNP symbol, and ashtrays, ties, scarves, car badges and other similar goods spread the symbol throughout Scotland as the Party grew from doorstep to doorstep.

A glance at my diary for 1965 and at my correspondence, committee minutes, etc., shows that life was very full. By this time, I had given up active Scouting, for it had been made clear to me after the 1964 Election result that a man who had become a comparatively successful candidate of the Scottish National Party was no longer acceptable as a County Commissioner. I got my marching orders in the nicest possible brotherly Scout way within a few weeks of the Election. After all my years of enthusiastic effort for the Scout Movement, my demotion was a bitter pill to swallow. It seemed that one could be a prominent Tory or Labour politician and still remain active at a senior level in the Scout Movement. However, I realised that the moves to get rid of me sprang from local enmity and not from Headquarters in Edinburgh or in London.

Some friends urged me to protest at the situation, but at the time it seemed too like fratricide to me to do anything of the sort and, in any case, I foresaw that my change of employment and my increased activity in the SNP would soon swallow up the time and energy which I had devoted to Scouting.

That is in fact what happened, and I entered a phase of intense non-stop activity which lasted for three years until 1st December 1967 when I was concussed in a road accident.

Fortunately, my health has always been good. I became a vegetarian at the end of 1964 and feel sure that the change enabled me to undertake more work than I had managed before.

Our family holiday in 1965 was spent on Bute, an island I know well. My mother was born in Rothesay, and I have visited it often throughout my life. We had good weather for our holiday, and we were accompanied by the daughter of one of my American cousins, Lisa who, at the age of sixteen, had a burning ambition to throw herself into the work of curing the racial and poverty problems of the U.S.A. In contrast, how simple were our problems here in Scotland—just to persuade people to believe in themselves and choose to have their own government.

As the Labour Government was hanging by a thread with a very slim majority, another General Election could not be far away and the SNP prepared in the autumn of 1965 to contest as many seats as possible. Robert McIntyre, the Convener of the Party's Election Committee, reckoned that if the Election was not held until the spring of 1966, we would be able to contest twenty-two or twenty-three seats. His prediction was fulfilled. We contested in twenty-three constituencies.

In 1965, the English political parties grudgingly agreed that the national parties of Wales and Scotland could each have, in that year, five minutes of television time and five minutes of sound radio time for Party Political Broadcasting in their own countries. This was not generosity but the direct result of a long campaign which built up pressure on the English parties from both Wales and Scotland.

That no further progress has been made, both parties still, in 1973, having only five minutes of television and five minutes of sound radio each year in spite of the obvious increase in the strength of both parties and the recorded increase in their support, reflects the deep-seated fear of the English parties that the national parties of Wales and Scotland might succeed in achieving their aims.

There is certainly no moral justification for preventing the free discussion on television and radio of political, social and economic ideas which are not immoral and which are propounded by political parties which are run democratically and enjoy a wide measure of support among the population.

Within this party political broadcasting issue, one can see the essential struggle by the Welsh and the Scots against continued English domination. The fact that this is maintained and supported by Welsh and Scottish off-shoots of English organisations, to a greater or lesser degree, only serves to highlight more clearly the basic questions—Is there a nation of Welsh and is there a nation of Scots? To those who answer "Yes," the next question is, "Are these nations to be allowed to continue to exist?" and if the answer to that question is "Yes," then one asks, "Why should these nations not be allowed to run their own affairs and to take part in the affairs of the British Isles, and in international affairs with the same rights as other nations?" The answer is that there is no valid reason, if the Welsh and Scots choose self-government.

The present English Tory Party is dominated by a man who has repeatedly used Disraeli's phrase, "one nation," for the various peoples of the British Isles for the last 25 years. When he first started propounding his ideas, Edward Heath was one of several showing leadership potential in the lower ranks of the Tory Party. Others were Enoch Powell, Reginald Maudling and Iain MacLeod—all men who could and did stand up and argue with Heath. At the time of writing, he is on his own, with little sign of a dissident voice within his Cabinet to disagree with him.

Mr Heath certainly produced an uncharacteristic departure from his "one nation" theory at the Scottish Tory Conference in Perth in 1968 when he proposed that there be a Scottish Assembly. This move in reaction to the growth of support for the Scottish National Party to nearly 40% of the electorate voting in the 1968 burgh elections was understandable. It was clearly a political move against the SNP who wished then and wish now that he would make it real and effective by setting up an elected Scottish Assembly. Such an Assembly would soon demand many things for Scotland, including full control over Scottish broadcasting.

The Labour Party is even more totally committed than the Tory Party to the "one nation" theory. In its Constitution and Standing Orders there is not the slightest token of recognition of the English, Welsh or Scottish nations. There is a reference to co-operation with the General Council of the T.U.C. but no

70

reference to the Scottish T.U.C. There is certainly no mention whatever of what is dressed up for public relations purposes by the Labour Party as a "Scottish Labour Party Conference" each year. A study of Labour Party handbooks, propaganda and manifestoes shows how totally English the organisation is. For example, in the same way as the Westminster Parliament often goes through English legislation changing "borough" to "burgh." etc., in order to produce legislation for Scotland, the Labour Party's book on the conduct of Local Elections in Scotland is a carelessly corrected version of the Labour Party's book on the conduct of Local Elections in England and Wales. The ridiculous mistakes are of no consequence in themselves but they reflect the acceptance by many people who became active in the Labour Party, of the total denial of the culture and history of Scotland.

Influenced by the Trade Union movement and by the Independent Labour Party in its earlier years, the Labour Party had favoured parliaments for Wales and Scotland, but the proportionately greater support given to the Labour Party in Wales and Scotland in comparison with England convinced the English leaders that they would not have much chance of forming a government in England alone, so in order to ensure the continued support of Scottish and Welsh Labour M.P.s in the English Parliament, proposals for self-government for Wales and Scotland were abandoned in the early 1930s. In fact, sentimental lip service was still paid to self-government until 1945 in order to retain votes. Since then, Labour Party spokesmen have been among the most vehement in opposition to self-government for Wales and Scotland.

However, in the Labour Movement in both Wales and Scotland, particularly in Wales, belief in the need for self-government has been maintained, and it was pressure from these elements in Wales, combined with elements of the National Party of Wales, Plaid Cymru, which forced the Labour and Tory Parties to capitulate and agree that there should be additional party political broadcasts in Wales and Scotland both during and between elections. This happened in March 1964.

The history of party political broadcasting goes back to 1947 when the Labour, Conservative and Liberal Parties and the B.B.C. agreed to confine opportunities for political broadcasting to parties contesting 50 seats at a General Election. This clearly reflected the "one nation" theory, as Plaid Cymru were totally excluded, having only 36 seats in Wales to contest.

71

In 1949, Lord Beveridge headed a Commission on Broadcasting which proposed that "there should be greater opportunity for political broadcasts both national in scope and limited to particular regions. It is essential in this to observe fair play in the quantity of facilities for debate, fair play meaning an opportunity for minorities to turn themselves into majorities. This is a matter on which we would like to see bold and varied experiments. Possibly the national commissions which we propose for the three national parts of the United Kingdom might make different experiments in this field."

The B.B.C. charter which followed the Report of the Beveridge Commission set up National Broadcasting Councils for Wales and for Scotland with responsibility for all broadcasting in their respective countries. The councils were to exercise their control "with full regard to the distinctive culture, interests, and tastes of our people in that country."

With the support of over 100 local authorities in Wales, Plaid Cymru made a claim for a share of party political broadcasting in Wales. The National Broadcasting Council for Wales agreed, called a meeting of party representatives in Wales and proposed to give each party, including Plaid Cymru, two programmes of 15 minutes each, every year.

The Conservative Postmaster-General at this time was Dr Charles Hill, subsequently Tory Minister of Propaganda as Minister without Portfolio, and now Lord Hill, who has been Chairman of the Independent Television Authority and Chairman of the B.B.C. After consulting the Labour and Tory Party leaders, Dr Hill told the National Broadcasting Council for Wales to drop their plans and that if they did not do so, he would invoke his power of veto to prevent them from being implemented. The National Broadcasting Council for Wales re-affirmed its belief in its plans and issued a statement to the effect that "they deeply deplore the attitude of the Leaders of the two main political parties in this matter." The governing body of the B.B.C. in London supported the Welsh Council. In July 1955, the Postmaster-General, Dr Hill, vetoed the plans. This is the only time since the B.B.C. was founded 50 years ago that the P.M.G.'s right to veto a B.B.C. decision has ever been invoked. The veto is of questionable legality but, of course, the Westminster government is judge and jury as well as lawmaker in this matter.

The "50 seat rule" was continued. The Scottish National Party had therefore to contest 70% of the 71 available seats while the U.K. parties needed only to fight 8% of their possible 630 constituencies. Plaid Cymru were left in the ridiculous position where, in order to get broadcasting time, they would have to fight fourteen seats outside Wales. Is it surprising that pirate radios came into action in both Wales and Scotland in order to broadcast the viewpoint of the two national parties? In this matter, Plaid Cymru had much wider support among organised official bodies than the SNP had in Scotland. Nevertheless, the Postmaster-General in 1961 refused to meet a delegation from Plaid Cymru to discuss the matter.

In 1962, yet another committee, the Pilkington Committee on Broadcasting, declared, "We are impressed by the widely representative nature of the submissions advocating party political broadcasts for Scotland and for Wales and recommend that the P.M.G.'s directive be amended to allow them on the understanding that they were to be additional to the broadcasts for the whole of the United Kingdom." The Government White Paper on the report said that this recommendation would be discussed "with the political parties, the B.B.C. and I.T.A." Plaid Cymru and the Scottish National Party were refused participation in the discussions. The P.M.G. told Plaid Cymru that the question was one for the Government as a whole and refused to answer them, so a letter was sent to the Prime Minister, Sir Alec Douglas Home. He referred it back to the P.M.G. Plaid Cymru wrote to Mr Harold Wilson, Leader of the Labour Party in 1963. His reply approved of the *status quo* continuing the 50 seat rule.

By May 1964 not only had the P.M.G.'s directive not been amended but all available time offered by the broadcasting authorities for the General Election had been divided by the three English parties amongst themselves.

However, cracks began to appear. In March, over 70 Welsh local authorities and many Trade Union District Committees, including the South Wales Area Committee of the N.U.M., had written to the leaders of the major parties to protest on behalf of Plaid Cymru. In Scotland, the SNP had secured written indication from the Scottish Unionists and Scottish Liberals that they supported the idea of a separate series of political broadcasts in Scotland; and Gordon Wilson and I had been received by the National Broadcasting Council of the B.B.C. for Scotland —we were the first delegation ever met by the Council in its ten-year span of office. We were assured that the Council intended to make specific proposals for a series of Scottish Party

Political Broadcasts and that the meeting to discuss their proposals would be held in London in July. It was suggested to us that we apply for representation at the meeting, at least for an opportunity to put our case.

We were not allowed to attend the meeting, nor have we ever been allowed to participate in any discussions whatsoever with the B.B.C., with I.T.A. or with the invisible and elusive people who represent the Labour, Tory and Liberal Parties in deciding how much time will be spent each year on political broadcasting and how it will be carved up.

The confusion as to who is really responsible can be noted in a letter dated 22nd July 1964, which I received from the Government (Tory) Chief Whip, Mr Martin Redmayne: "Incidentally, may I say in relation to general election broadcasts, so far as eligibility for a national broadcast is concerned, formal responsibility rests with the Broadcasting Authorities although the qualifications which must be met before minor parties are allotted a national broadcast is a matter which has been discussed and agreed at successive meetings with the parties which decide the general election arrangements." It seems likely that at the July meeting before that letter was sent to me, the Tory, Labour and Liberal Parties had agreed to support new arrangements subject to three conditions: —

1. That any broadcasts would be in addition to the General Election series for the whole of Britain.

2. That they would be broadcast simultaneously by B.B.C. and I.T.A.

3. That their allocation during an election campaign be determined by the number of candidates in the field on nomination day, and between elections by the total vote cast for each party in the previous general election.

Well, we did not get a broadcast for the 1964 General Election, but the pressure from Wales and Scotland had resulted in a concession with regard to political discussion programmes leading up to the General Election. B.B.C. and I.T.A. introduced a rule that they would allow participation to parties contesting 20% or more of the seats within each "regional" area. That is why it was urgent for us in Scotland to contest 15 seats in 1964—so that we could have representatives on the discussion programmes.

In fact, S.T.V. gave us the best opportunity of all in these programmes by allowing each representative five minutes in which to put his or her case, prior to the discussion. I went into the Theatre Royal Studios in Glasgow prepared to give what was, in effect, a five-minute party political broadcast. I went armed with "props" in the shape of figures about unemployment, emigration and the cost of subsidising England, and S.T.V. kindly put these on the screen at the appropriate times when I was speaking. Some of the participants of other parties in the programme were furious that I had made such effective use of the time allotted. The fact that this was one of our very few opportunities, compared with the many available to themselves, did not strike them as being either unfair or undemocratic—such is the corruption of power.

In 1965, after much activity by Gordon Wilson, who has been the Scottish National Party's most effective and persistent representative in this battle on the party political broadcasting front, we were told that we would have five minutes on television and five minutes on sound. We elected to take our television broadcast in September and our sound broadcast on St Andrew's Day, and the National Executive Committee appointed Arthur Donaldson and myself to make the sound and television broadcasts respectively.

We used the opportunity, on 29 September 1965, to launch our membership recruitment drive for that autumn. Several SNP Branches publicised the fact that we were getting our first broadcast and endeavoured to make use of the publicity in order to help recruitment efforts. At National Council in December, Arthur Donaldson reported that the television appearance had been seen and heard by over $1\frac{1}{4}$ million people and the favourable reaction was reflected in the report by Robert McIntyre that over 1,200 written enquiries for membership and information had been received within four days of the broadcast, which had ended with the following appeal: —

"If your home is here, Scotland is your country. We want you to have a secure place in it and a sense of achievement in its democratic self-government. I ask you to put your faith in Scotland as we do; to join our ranks; and to vote SNP when given the chance. We have the men and women and skills to make Scotland a country to be proud of. We know that the vast majority of Scots want a Scottish Parliament. With a strong and united will to shoulder our responsibilities, we will take our place among the nations. Your first loyalty is to Scotland. You can choose such a future. It is up to you to put Scotland first. Write to us tonight and we will send you details of Scotland's Democratic Party."

I repeated our address and it appeared on vision before I said goodnight at the end of my 650 words.

The novelty of the SNP having a broadcast and the good publicity build-up given to it ensured to a large extent the response we received.

It is over seven years since that first broadcast of five minutes, and we still have an allowance of only five minutes. That it is the very antithesis of democratic free speech for us to be so restricted is clear to any objective observer. In Parliament, Winifred Ewing, Gwynfor Evans and Donald Stewart have carried on the sparring match with shadows. Mrs Ewing was told, after repeated questioning, that it was not a Parliamentary matter, although the correspondent who had dealt with us on this subject had invariably been the Government Chief Whip.

After the 1970 General Election, Donald Stewart took the case to the Ombudsman. At first it looked as though he was going to deal with the matter, but after several months of delay he replied saying that it was the responsibilty of the Postmaster General. Going back to Parliament with the question, Donald Stewart has been given the same elusive and unsatisfactory answers we have always had.

Official Party Political Broadcast time is important, but it is not the most important aspect of the use of broadcasting, particularly television. Because we are allowed only five minutes, the broadcasting authorities can justify ignoring us almost completely at such times as the vital two or three-week period prior to a General Election, as was done in both 1966 and 1970.

The real implication of the ban is an attitude which says that the Welsh and Scottish nations do not exist. You must be English before you can rate for a reasonably fair allocation of time on television to put across your political viewpoint. In my view, we have been patient too long. If anything is a "civil rights" issue, it is the right to free speech, the right, as Lord Beveridge's Commission said, "for minorities to turn themselves into majorities."

The Scottish National M.P. for the Western Isles, Donald Stewart, is on record as having warned the House of Commons that this restrictive practice will not be tolerated for ever.

76

CHAPTER 6

MOVEMENT ON THE MOVE, 1966-67

AT THE START of 1966, the Party's Headquarters arrangements were under stress. There were still only two Executive Vice-Chairman, Douglas Drysdale and myself. Rosemary Hall was very heavily engaged at the Edinburgh Office and Ian Macdonald, based in the Glasgow Office, was spending a great deal of time travelling around the country helping to build up the Party organisation. New branches were coming into existence at the rate of at least one each week at this time. Gordon Wilson, as National Secretary (an honorary post) had a tremendous output of letters, etc., which was dealt with in the Glasgow Office. Douglas Drysdale and I both had part-time secretaries. Altogether, a lot of work was being done, but re-organisation was clearly essential if we were to cope efficiently with the Party's growth.

The National Executive Committee gave Douglas Drysdale the job of examining the situation and suggesting changes to improve it. He made a thorough examination and submitted a report on the organisational and financial arrangements. A special meeting of the Executive was held in January to consider his report along with representations from other members of the Executive, including a memorandum from William Johnston, the Convener of the Association of Scottish Nationalist Trade Unionists. Among the proposals which he made was one that the Party Chairman should hold office for one year only and should not be eligible for re-election, and that the full-time professional staff be increased. There is no doubt that there is merit in these suggestions. My own idea on the chairmanship, dating back to 1962, was that the Chairman should be employed on a full-time basis by the Party.

The underlying wish in both cases was that the Party should have one or more full-time professional executives to manage its organisational affairs, and William Johnston's proposals had the additional merit of ensuring that little or no "empire-building" could be done by the Chairman. From my experience as a member of the Executive and as Chairman, the accepted methods of operation of the Party, with monthly meetings of the Executive Committee and diffusion of executive responsibility, do not provide conditions in which empire-building would be easy should any occupant of the chair wish to do so.

The Executive decided to recommend to National Conference that the number of Executive Vice-Chairmen be increased to four, and that their duties be allocated by National Council. The Executive also authorised a considerable amount of re-organisation between the Edinburgh and Glasgow offices, shifting a large proportion of the administrative load to Edinburgh, where Rosemary Hall took over a few weeks later as Organising Secretary, a new post which gave her talents even greater scope. Alasdair Macdonald, a Glasgow minister, was appointed part-time Public Relations Officer and the P.R. work was transferred to the Glasgow office.

My own life was as hectic as usual at this time. The long awaited debate between Tam Dalyell, Labour M.P. for West Lothian, and myself as representative of the Scottish National Party, took place in Linlithgow on 5th February with Professor Esmond Wright as Chairman. The origins of this particular challenge were in the SNP's party political broadcast on 29th September 1965, in which I had said, "Scotland, in spite of her problems, gives considerable financial aid to England." Tam Dalyell had said in public that the Scottish National Party should not say such things. Glasgow Area Council of the SNP then challenged Mr Dalyell to prove, in a formal debate with a neutral Chairman, that Scotland did not subsidise England financially. Tam Dalyell accepted the challenge, although at the time he was a member of the Labour Government, being a Private Parliamentary Secretary. He could not, or would not, find a seconder, and he stipulated that the debate must take place in West Lothian. Before the debate took place he resigned from the Government.

A great deal of research was done by the SNP in preparing for this debate and a useful by-product was a duplicated booklet, *Scotland's Subsidy to England*. Mr Dalyell produced absolutely nothing to weaken our arguments and estimates, in spite of having had the privilege of choosing the date and the advantages of being a member of the Government, and having Government and Labour Party resources available for nearly four months of preparation.

However, it was a useful run-in to the General Election which was announced at the end of February. We fielded 23 candidates and increased our vote to 124,000. Some of the 23 constituencies were ill-prepared in organisation and short of money. Headquarters could do very little to help them financially.

Our Election Manifesto put jobs at the head of the list—"In the ten years to 1964, England's net addition of jobs for men was 903,000 while Scotland's net loss of jobs for men was 34,000."

At this time, policy was still drafted on an *ad hoc* basis and *SNP and You* was still our basic policy document, but the manifesto showed considerable development of policies since 1964. For the assistance of candidates we produced a series of "Broadsheets," dealing with such things as an analysis of the Labour Party's so-called Scottish Plan for 1965-1970 which was published early in 1966. The Plan stated that at least 130,000 new jobs would have to be created, yet just before it was published, another Government statement withdrew the investment incentives from the service industries in Scotland and excluded the whole of the Edinburgh area from development status. As we now know the results of the Wilson Labour Government's attempts to implement this Plan and its English counterpart, all I need to point out is that during Labour's six-year "reign of terror" the number of jobs for men in Scotland was *reduced* by 64,000. This was done by the Party which claims to represent the workers of Scotland. They doubled our loss of jobs in half the time the Tories had previously taken.

Other broadsheets dealt with the subsidies to England (the fruits of the debate with Dalyell), a National Health Service for Scotland, shipbuilding, engineering, agriculture, forestry, education and so on. In this election campaign, the SNP candidates received more help from Headquarters than their predecessors had ever had in previous elections. At last, we were beginning to look like a really national party, able, within the foreseeable future, to contest all the seats in Scotland.

Ian Macdonald, and quite a few other spokesmen at national level, forecast publicly that we would be in a position to contest all the seats in Scotland by the next General Election in 1970 or 1971. Though this was severely frowned on by some members, my own belief was that it did not make much difference to people's support whether they knew we were going to fight every seat or not—just having candidates is not really an adequate sign on its own, of a party's strength, at least not the kind of strength which gives people confidence to vote for it in sufficient numbers to give a majority.

79

Our results were certainly encouraging. We won more than 10% of the vote in 16 of the 23 constituencies, including four in which our share was more than 20%. West Lothian was still in the lead with 35·3%—nearly 18,000 votes. Robert McIntyre had fought a wonderful campaign in West Stirlingshire. From a "standing start," and only three or four weeks of campaigning, he scored 26% of the vote, coming second. Arthur Donaldson collected over 20% of the vote in Kinross and West Perthshire, and Douglas Drysdale polled a similar percentage in Clackmannanshire and East Stirlingshire.

The geographical concentration of our contests was still predominantly central, the other constituencies in which we won over 10% of the vote being East Fife; West Fife; Dunfermline; Kirkcaldy; Midlothian; Stirling, Falkirk and Grangemouth; Perth and East Perthshire; West Dumbartonshire; Shettleston (Glasgow); Maryhill (Glasgow); and Dumfriesshire.

With the exception of East Aberdeenshire, the other seats we fought were in Central Scotland—East Dumbartonshire, Rutherglen, four in Glasgow and one in Edinburgh.

In spite of the high figure polled by the SNP in West Lothian, many of the activists there were bitterly disappointed that we did not win. Many had been sure that we would. The local Labour Party leadership had clearly been in a panic, but the Labour vote in West Lothian remained pretty solid. It did not much matter to Labour how they retained their solidarity: in elections there is only one winner and there are no prizes or garlands for the runners-up.

The Labour Party used their familiar stock of lies in order to discourage people from voting SNP. We were attacked so viciously in leaflets that we sought Counsel's opinion on them. The accusations were scurrilous and untrue, but after taking advice we decided that we just had to take such knocks as part of the cost of winning votes.

For the first time in an election campaign, bitter and even vitriolic hostility was stirred up against us at meetings and on occasions when parties of canvassers from the Labour Party met canvassers from the SNP. The persistent organised heckling from the Labour Party supporters was mainly on the possible use of force in the struggle for self-government. There are undoubtedly circumstances in which civil disobedience campaigns and demonstrations are desirable and even necessary, and in which they can be effective in shifting public, parliamentary and government opinion, but the use of violence in order to convince the people of Scotland to vote for self-government is totally unacceptable. What the Labour Party hecklers tried and failed to do was to undermine our stand on non-violence and our reliance on democratic procedures.

However, the election had its light side as well. We had some unusual and amusing excitement at one stage when Ladbroke's, the London bookies, following the initiative of some Labour Party people in Bo'ness, offered 1000-1 against the SNP winning in West Lothian. After this appeared in a local paper, we tried to put some money on at these odds, but they were promptly shortened to 10-1 against and to even shorter odds by polling day.

The result of that election left me with a sense of regret which has never quite disappeared. The 1970 General Election results, especially in Hamilton, provoked a similar feeling. Until 1966, I had never experienced hysterical hatred of fellow Scots expressed against the party which stands for the virtues and morality of freedom. Political debate is one thing, but the dishonest rousing of emotions by feeding ignorance with lies about our patriotic and humanitarian hopes and wishes for our fellow citizens is quite another. In the General Election of 1970 such tactics were used in Hamilton as well as in West Lothian and other places. However, in his letter of congratulation, Arthur Donaldson encouraged us to take heart from the reaction of the Labour Party. "They are obviously getting scared," he wrote, "this time we were biting hard and West Lothian has borne the brunt again."

After the election, Ian Macdonald's report to the Executive was a concise argument in support of his optimistic forecast that we would fight all the seats in Scotland in an election in 1970 or 1971. Events, of course, justified his forecast. Alasdair MacDonald took up his appointment as P.R.O. on the day the election was announced so he had quite a baptism of fire. He was on a part-time basis, having been asked originally to work only about 10 hours a week, although Rosemary Hall had been spending sometimes 10 hours a day and more on such work. It was quite clear that the new arrangement would be inadequate.

My experiences as a candidate in three elections, and the great value I had found in drawing upon the results of research work, led me to make two proposals, the first being the appointment of a Research Officer as soon as possible. What I had in mind was "someone with a degree or a professional qualification or training in accounting, economics, journalism or the law, possibly someone in their late 20s who was politically aware and who had already committed himself or herself to the aims and policies of the SNP." The other suggestion was for the production of a "Candidate's Handbook," the subject matter to be mainly statistics, sources and quotations for use in speeches, leaflets, etc. Its main purpose would be "to provide candidates with information on the economic and social state of Scotland; the promises and performances of the other parties; and the cost and method of carrying out our own proposals and policies." The second proposal had to await fulfilment of the first for its implementation, and it was Donald Bain, appointed Research Officer in August 1968, who produced *Scotland—Facts and Comparisons,* which constituted the kind of handbook I had in mind in 1966.

Other points which I put to the Executive in April 1966 were the necessity for thorough preparation for contesting as many county council seats as possible in 1967, similar preparations for the burghs, and the drafting of a series of radical policies for Scotland. I also put up for discussion the suggestion that the National Conference should consider the possibility of changing or adding to the title of the Party in order to put less emphasis on nationalism and more on democracy. This was quite clearly a reaction to the West Lothian experiences in the recent general election campaign.

To the following meeting of the Executive in May, I added some further suggestions which were more concerned with long-term plans. I believed that "we should expand our aims to include a more clearly defined outline of the social and economic pattern which we envisage as being best for Scotland in the future." In fact, this has still not been done formally within the constitution, although plans approved by the Party after the 1970 General Election do include expanded aims.

I suggested that before the next General Election it would be necessary for us "to make definite proposals regarding a constitution for Scotland and all the things which will follow, *e.g.* all the arrangements necessary to enable a Scottish Government to control effectively the finance and economy of the country. This will include proposals for banking arrangements in trading with England in particular and with other countries in general." I linked these matters with the possibility of the U.K. entering the Common Market.

The development of policies in the social, economic and political fields which are of topical interest as well as those which will be of long term interest for an independent Scotland were also urged in my report—particularly those concerning local authorities and their work, because I believed it essential for the SNP to participate fully in local authority elections. I saw this as a natural development of the growth of the influence of the Party as more and more people concerned with the communities in which they lived saw membership of the SNP as a means of constructive participation; and also as existing members of the Party saw local authority work as a practical expression of their belief in self-government and of their willingness to identify with the needs and aspirations of the people of their communities.

I re-iterated my belief that the Party need not be so obviously nationalist because I believed that about 90% of the people of Scotland were already nationalist and did not require to be made particularly conscious of the fact. I wrote in my report, "Basically, we have to answer two questions—1, Will Scotland be prosperous and secure with a government of our own? and 2, Can the SNP show that it has the policies and the men and women to lead an independent Scotland in an efficient and democratic way?"

As far as organisation was concerned, I anticipated development on lines similar to those which had taken place in the previous two or three years, with a strengthening of constituency associations. At national level, I envisaged more pressure on our semi-professional political leadership (the National Executive Committee) with an increasing need for high calibre full-time administrators, possibly office-bearers, elected by National Conference or National Council. Most of these matters were dealt with in succeeding months and years. The proposal about change of name came too late for the 1966 Conference and it has not been revived.

My morale and that of the Party received a boost after the General Election when I was elected the first Honorary President of the Students' Association by the students of the newly constituted Heriot-Watt University. This was a position equivalent to that of Rector in the older Scottish Universities, with a place on the University Court. Before standing for election, I had to give an undertaking that I would attend regularly to my duties. In fact, at the end of my three-year term, by which time I had got to know the ways of the University, I recommended to the Students' Association that they find someone who could give about 10 hours a week to the job because it was very time-consuming to do it properly.

ILLUSTRATIONS

84

My installation did not take place until February 1967. I would have said that the main contents of my speech were predictable but the reception I got from students and staff and the resulting press coverage were better than I had expected. For the first time since the result of the 1962 by-election, what I said was given prominent front-page coverage. The *Weekly Scotsman* gave headlines with emphasis on what they saw as an extraordinary occasion—"extraordinary that Mr Wolfe should have been so outspoken while holding such high office from the platform of such a famous and dignified University, extraordinary that it should have been received so warmly by senior dignitaries of the University."

In my direct references to Scotland I said, "What I seek for you and for your University and for Scotland is not just restoration but renaissance. For too long, we Scots have had to be satisfied with second-rate or worse in many spheres. Third-rate government is something to which we are so accustomed that we do not realise how bad it is, and in saying that I do not refer to those who administer Westminster's decisions in Scotland but to those who sit in that over-crowded and over-rated building on the left bank of the Thames.

"There is no doubt that a political renaissance is badly needed in Scotland. I believe that it is the only source which can lead to the solution of much of what is wrong in Scotland today. Fortunately, the renaissance has started and is gathering momentum at a rate which will gain it the support of the majority of Scots within a few years.

"We do not want simply a restoration to the pre-eminent position which Scotland held 50 years ago in many spheres, including education. We want to use our resources to develop our industries and to provide for the education of our people in order to make the Scotland of the future, not only of the past, a place of which we can be proud—a place in which all will want to stay, in contrast to the present necessity for so many to emigrate in order to find work; a place in which the democratic Scottish tradition is fostered and developed not only for our own contentment and prosperity but to enable us to play our part in Europe and in the world.

"There is no clash in a democratic country between love of one's native land, and love of freedom and humanity. For Scotland it is the eleventh hour, because if we are taken into the European Common Market as a region of Greater England before having at least a handful of Scottish National Party

Members of Parliament at Westminster as evidence of the Scottish political renaissance, it will be much more difficult for us to fight our way to a position of freedom and dignity and effectiveness.

"I believe that the people of Scotland can make a distinctive contribution in world affairs if we have the will to go forward in independence. Not only can we contribute to scientific and economic progress, but in the kind of egalitarian outlook which has permeated Scotland for more than 1000 years we have a source of possible contributions to world society and international diplomacy. I believe that as a nation we can play a part in the evolutionary convergence of mankind towards a brotherhood in which peace is the accepted universal basis of society."

The Party started its 1966 - 67 year in good heart. It now had four Executive Vice-Chairmen as had been envisaged eighteen months earlier. They were Douglas Drysdale, responsible for Finance; James Lees, in charge of Organisation; John Gair, with responsibility for Policy; and James Braid to deal with Publicity. I was elected Senior Vice-Chairman and it was arranged that I would be responsible for what was later called the Economics and Information Department. With the need for a lot of hard work to build up Chieftain Forge Ltd. as a specialist firm dealing in tools and machinery for forestry, I had realised before Conference that I would not have as much time as before for Party work so I had declined to accept nomination as an Executive Vice-Chairman.

Business travels abroad that year, on three separate occasions, each to a different country—Finland, Sweden and Norway—stimulated my imagination as to what the people of Scotland could achieve with self-government, and I also picked up a lot of useful ideas for producing comparative statistics for the proposed and much needed "Candidate's Handbook." My visits to these countries in Northern Europe had a primary purpose of seeking out manufacturers whom Chieftain Forge Ltd. could represent in the British Isles. Our first contacts were in Finland, which proved to be fortunate because Finland's manufacturers offered more items of equipment likely to be of use in the British Isles than their counterparts in either Sweden or Norway. By the end of the year, we were representing three Norwegian and five Finnish firms.

Finland had interested me before I visited it. George Wolfe & Sons Ltd., with whom I had been employed from 1952 - 64, had supplied thousands of tons of steel to Finland in that period, so I knew something about the country and had been favourably impressed. My visit heightened my regard and my fascination. Finland has a population smaller than Scotland. It was totally "down and out" after the end of the Second World War, with no allies and in the unenviable position of trying to maintain independence and freedom with a Western European type of constitution while sharing a thousand miles of border with Soviet Russia.

Finland had won its own independence only 30 years earlier. In some ways, it was a very young country. Its industrial development was generations behind that of most Western European countries. Russia had taken, as part of war reparations, the province of Karelia, whose 400,000 inhabitants had elected to remain Finnish citizens and had thus had to settle in other parts of Finland. Think what it would have been like in Scotland if, immediately after the end of World War II, with shortage and rationing, we had suddenly had to absorb an increased population of half a million. The Finns had very little to share other than land and forest, but they did it.

At the time of my visit to Finland in 1966, the sorry state I have just described had existed less than twenty years earlier. I certainly did not find a paradise, but in many ways it was much closer to one than Scotland was—Scotland with far greater wealth; Scotland with the possibility of diplomatic and trading friends all over the world based on existing connections; Scotland with a well-educated and mainly industrialised population; Scotland with the best airfield in Western Europe for trans-Atlantic journeys, and so on. I could go on and on comparing Scotland in the late 1940s with Finland at the same period. There would be no real comparison. It would be like comparing two players in a game of cards with one holding almost all the face cards and all the trumps.

Yet in 1966, the standard of living in Finland was as high as that in Scotland. There were no slums in Finland. Emigration had taken place but it had never been nearly so serious as emigration from Scotland. Finland had received no foreign aid in the late '40s and in the 1950s, but it had paid immense sums in gold to Russia. Industrialisation had made spectacular progress based on Finnish resources, and a rule that foreign investment was limited to 49% of an enterprise.

The Finns built ships for themselves and for others; also paper-making machinery, forestry machinery, furniture and countless other sophisticated exports. Finland had a world-renowned air service—Finnair—which was profitable (this reminds me that Tam Dalyell once publicly rebuked me for saying that Scotland could maintain its own airline. He said that Scotland was not big enough. He obviously had not heard of Finnair or Aer Lingus).

The Finnish people, whatever their origins (about 10% of them are of Swedish origin) really believe in Finland and in their power to run their own country. These are their aces—their will power and their Parliament. The results are not only the economic benefits of a progressive economy; they clearly put high values on beauty and good design in buildings, clothes, town planning and furniture, as well as in the arts and crafts, some of which, such as glass-making and jewellery, have become highly profitable export industries.

Another point to bear in mind is that Finland has winter for seven months of the year. I have visited a farm comparatively near the Arctic Circle where wonderful crops of barley are grown, thanks to the power of the sun and to the ingenuity of man—Finnish man.

Now, in 1973, the gross national product of the Finns is beyond that not only of Scotland, but of the United Kingdom. They have done well nationally, and have certainly played a significant part in international humanitarian affairs, having pursued a path of neutrality and honour between the Communist power bloc and the United States power bloc. Their artists, sportsmen, designers, architects and engineers have world-wide reputations for leadership and integrity.

If Finland can do it, Scotland can do it. If the Scots have the will, as the Finns have the will, they *will* do it. The Finns have had inflation, strikes and other industrial troubles. They have their own armed forces to support. They have problems similar to ours and Finland is not, as I said, a paradise, but the people of Finland are infinitely better off in terms of human fulfilment than we are.

If Scotland had won self-government after the Second World War and had achieved economic growth rates comparable with those of Finland, we could have been better off now than we would be if we had all the projected oil revenues flowing into a Scottish Treasury; and I am sure that we would have played a significant part in the struggle for world peace.

Sweden and Norway have similar lessons to teach us but neither country was in such a disadvantageous position as

Finland 25 years ago. The lesson is clear. The statements of the Westminster politicians, particularly those who represent English parties in Scotland, about Scotland being too small and too poor to support self-government are utter rubbish. They cannot possibly be spoken in ignorance. They can only be spoken in deceit, deliberately, diabolically and selfishly in their own interests.

One of the products of the rise of the Scottish National Party in 1966 was the "Scottish Self-Government Bill" introduced by the Liberal M.P. for Inverness-shire, Russell Johnston, who wore his kilt for the occasion, much to the derisive amusement of many of his fellow M.P.s. Appropriately enough, it was ordered by the House of Commons to be printed on St Andrew's Day, but there was little else of real Scottish significance in it as far as the English M.P.s were concerned; and, of course, the House of Commons rejected it as so much waste paper, like its many predecessors, the last one of which had been the "Government of Scotland Bill" of 1926. In fact, the rejection of the 1926 Bill had been one of the important contributory factors in the founding of the National Party of Scotland in 1928, which became the Scottish National Party in 1932 after amalgamating with the Scottish Party. The only way to make a Scottish Self-Government Bill effective is to have a majority of the M.P.s from Scotland committed to it and committed to abandon Westminster and set up a provisional Government in Scotland if the House of Commons refuses to take reasonable steps to establish an independent parliament in Scotland.

It is quite conceivable, of course, that the English House of Commons might take such steps before a majority of the M.P.s from Scotland are representative of a party fully committed to self-government for Scotland. The point is that major steps towards the establishment of a Scottish Parliament require democratic support from the electorate. That the Scottish National Party will get such support in due course, I have no doubt. In 1968, for example, nearly 40% of the hundreds of thousands of Scots who voted in the burgh elections voted for the Scottish National Party. That is an indication of the kind of swing which is possible in Scotland, and the limit is by no means set at 40%. At least 75% of the people of Scotland want self-government but they wish some pre-requisites to be met before they will vote for it. It is up to the SNP to meet these requirements. 1966 saw progress towards doing that.

Probably the most important indication of progress towards self-government in 1966 came from Wales. There are many

89

reasons why the national parties of Wales and Scotland must each campaign separately for very similar aims, but there is no doubt that the progress of one assists the progress of the other, and the return in a by-election in Carmarthen of Gwynfor Evans, the President of Plaid Cymru, certainly boosted the morale and helped the progress of the Scottish National Party. Although the election of a Plaid Cymru or an SNP member to Westminster is a kind of sentence of banishment which has to be enthusiastically tholed and taken advantage of, it is, of course, a reward for effort, and in the case of Gwynfor Evans, it was certainly just reward.

Gwynfor Evans is a great man, loved and respected by hundreds of thousands of his compatriots. He is a man of many parts—a barrister by training; a farmer and market gardener in practice. His love of Wales shows in all his activities—as a leader in the Christian Church in his land, as a scholar, writer and speaker, as a County Councillor (since 1945), and as a much travelled internationalist and pacifist known in many countries throughout the world.

At the General Election in March, the Labour Party candidate had been elected with a majority of 9,233, the Liberal candidate having been second with 11,988, and Gwynfor Evans had come third with 7,416. Exactly 15 weeks later, on 14th July, Gwynfor Evans won the seat with a majority of 2,346. Naturally, the SNP was overjoyed and the *Scots Independent,* in welcoming the result, said prophetically, "There are few safe seats left for Labour or Tory in Scotland. The first by-election in Scotland will prove it."

Gwynfor came to Scotland in October to speak at meetings in Glasgow, Aberdeen and Edinburgh. Thousands came to hear him and gave him standing ovations. His basic theme in his speeches was the importance of nationhood.

It is a basic fact of human life, he said. "We are separate nations . . . we have more in common than that which divides us but the differences are important because they do something to enrich our life and the life of the world. A nation is a community, a society with certain characteristics performing a most important function—the transmission from one generation to another down the centuries of values which have been found to be good and true in our lives together. This education which is given by national traditions to all of us in human values is the most important education any of us ever gets. This should comprehend all formal education as it is the basis of civilisation.

"A nation cannot live without national freedom just as it is impossible for a man or woman to live a full life unless he or she is free. A slave may have the best treatment in the world but, if he lacks freedom, he can never fully be a human being. It is equally true to say the same of the human communities we call nations. The nation is the basic community on which world order rests. There is no other possible moral basis for international order. Wales and Scotland have something to do in the world scene but we can do nothing. The English Parliament in London makes use of us. It disposes of our wealth, it feeds on our moral support—for example, it assumed that we were behind the Labour Government in the obscenity of a war in Vietnam. We ought to be in a position to express our own attitudes to such matters. There are smaller, less experienced communities than ours who are in a position to do that—over 30 member states of U.N.O. are smaller than Wales and over 50 have smaller populations than Scotland."

Gwynfor Evans concluded: "It is high time that the people of Scotland insisted on doing their duty as a nation and taking their due place in the life of the world. Their due place is in the van of nations—not in the dim, grey provincial existence of the British state. There is no such thing as a British nation. A British state—yes —but a British nation is a creature of a state. There are four nations in these islands. This is a multi-nation state but this fact is ignored completely by the English Parliament from which our Governments are formed. The people of Scotland must now take their country seriously."

Gwynfor Evans' visit was the signal for the SNP's autumn recruitment drive. Enthusiastic activity went on all over Scotland, almost entirely by people without previous active experience in a political party. The belief in nationhood which Gwynfor Evans and many others expressed, spread throughout the people of Scotland. New members were recruited sometimes at the rate of over 1000 a week and new branches were formed, especially in those parts of the country in which we previously had no organisation at all.

There was one constituency in particular, with a long record of SNP activity, in which the recruitment drive had a special significance because of rumours that the age and length of service of the sitting Labour M.P. qualified him for entry to the House of Lords or for the Chairmanship of some suitable Board or Corporation. The constituency was Hamilton in which the Party had been active for 20 years or more. It had been contested with David Rollo as candidate in 1959 and although it had not been contested since, there was a small group of dedicated members. On 31st August 1966, they adopted Mrs Winifred Ewing, a Glasgow solicitor, as prospective candidate. As one of the speakers at the meeting, I met her for the first time, although our paths had very nearly crossed many times before in the Party and in the Saltire Society.

In spite of Gwynfor Evans' victory in Carmarthen, the thought of tackling and winning Hamilton was daunting. It was about the safest seat for Labour in Scotland and had been retained in March 1966 with a majority of 16,576, in a straight fight with a Conservative candidate. Our campaign started in Hamilton in the autumn of 1966. Meanwhile, significant things were happening in other parts of Scotland.

A municipal by-election in the Ruchill ward of Glasgow in October had a very close result. The SNP candidate was one of the most loyal and hard-working members of the Party— Hugh Macdonald, a Gaelic-speaking Glaswegian who personifies the fire, integrity and courtesy of the ideal Scot. If Labour had lost another twenty-five votes to the SNP, Hugh Macdonald would have won the seat. One of the features of this election and its result was the point noted at the time by several journalists that both the Tory and Labour parties would prefer to concede victory to each other rather than risk letting the SNP win. This kind of fraternising between Tory and Labour became common. These pseudo-Scots kissed and hugged each other at results in which they defeated the party which stands for the dignity and freedom of independence for Scotland.

The Carmarthen result, the visit of Gwynfor Evans, the Ruchill result and an SNP win in a Stirling County Council by-election at the end of October all strengthened the morale of the Party throughout Scotland, so that when Hogmanay ushered in the prospect of a by-election at Pollok in Glasgow, the Party looked ahead with great optimism.

The by-election was caused by the death of the Labour member who had won the seat for Labour in 1964, wiping out a large Tory majority; his majority in 1966 had been 1,975. The seat had been Tory for 46 years before Alex Garrow had won it for Labour. The SNP candidate was the first one named in the contest, George Leslie, a veterinary surgeon, aged 30, who had stood for the Party in 1966 in Craigton, next door to Pollok. The Tory candidate provided a surprise; he was Professor Esmond Wright, an Englishman in the History Department of Glasgow University who, most people in Scotland thought, was quite neutral in politics, as he had been such an acceptable chairman of so many television discussion programmes on current affairs.

The national press showed considerable interest in the Pollok by-election and in the SNP candidate. The publicity climate was totally different to that in which I had fought West Lothian in 1962, when there was little or no national coverage of the contest. In Pollok, our resources to cope with the attentions of the press were inadequate and there was insufficient co-ordination of policy. This was an understandable result of shortage of professional staff and lack of experience, wedded to tremendous and almost overwhelming enthusiasm and optimism. I have often remarked that the people of Glasgow are less emotionally inhibited than Scots elsewhere, and this shows in what sometimes appears to outsiders to be an irrational and sentimentalist approach by members of all parties in Glasgow to political discussion. Pollok was no exception and the intervention of a Liberal candidate contributed to the warmth of the debate.

The Liberals chose a candidate who was a Marketing Executive with a soap firm. This was quite appropriate and the Liberals used the usual boastful brand of soft soap in their campaign, getting headlines like "Scot Nats will lose deposit— Liberals." This was quoting Liberal Party Chairman George Mackie, who said, "Our figures show that the SNP will lose their deposit as they are at the bottom in this election." The Liberal candidate had both Russell Johnston, M.P. for Inverness-shire, and the new English Liberal Party Leader, Jeremy Thorpe, to speak for him; but as the campaign progressed, their trumpetings became squeaks and the press eventually ignored them, as did the voters—only 735 out of nearly 40,000 voted Liberal.

The SNP attracted workers to this by-election fight from all over Scotland. When it became obvious to us that the result would be close, with Labour, Tory and SNP all collecting about 30% of the poll, I publicly asked the Liberal candidate to stand down "for the sake of the future of the people of Scotland." I said, "You must know you have not the slightest chance of winning Pollok and you must know that George Leslie could win with the support he now has." The Liberals hadn't the wit or the humility to see that their votes could have made a difference. In fact, George Leslie would still have been third, but we hadn't estimated that the Liberal would get so few; if he had stood down, the SNP's chances would have appeared more credible and George Leslie would have had a very good chance of benefiting by more votes than those eventually cast for the Liberal.

The Labour Party was fighting a sticky campaign because of the unpopularity of the Labour Government at this time. They produced Government authorisation for the Clyde Port Authority to build a container port at Greenock on the eve of the election, and chose the eve of poll for a party political broadcast by the Scottish Secretary, Mr William Ross, in order to try and retain the seat.

George Leslie's poll in Pollok, nearly 11,000 votes and over 28%, on the first occasion on which the SNP had fought the seat, once again showed the possibilities. Partly because there was so much national press publicity for the by-election, some SNP spokesmen tended to be rather too optimistic in their claims in the last stages of the campaign. I agreed with the criticism of this, as I am sure that expressions of quiet confidence do not lose votes and probably gain more than specifically-worded claims which seem to reflect more showmanship than responsibility.

Our friends in Wales had also done well on the same day, at the by-election in Rhondda West where the Plaid Cymru candidate, Victor Davies, had come second with 40%, reducing Labour's majority from 16,888 (in March 1966) to 2,306. The Welsh and the Scottish National Parties took great encouragement from the results. Few political commentators anywhere saw any lasting significance in them.

Within the Liberal Party in Scotland, the humiliation of the Liberal vote in Pollok produced ructions. Mr Ludovic Kennedy produced a resolution for the Liberal Party urging co-operation with the SNP and Mr James Davidson, Liberal M.P. for West Aberdeenshire, made an independent approach to the S.N.P. The Liberals themselves rejected Ludovic Kennedy's plea quite emphatically and the conditions of Mr Davidson's offer made it impossible for the SNP to accept.

My plea to the Liberal candidate, David Miller, to withdraw was made with complete sincerity in the belief that his withdrawal would be of benefit to Scotland. I did not have much hope for success because of the rather arrogant attitude to the SNP of the Liberals' Chairman, Mr George Mackie, and because of the virulent anti-SNP campaign which the Liberal agent, Mr Arthur Purdom, had waged in Pollok, as he had done in West Lothian in 1962 and in various other contests.

My letter to David Miller highlighted the illogicality of the Liberal position which, in 1973, still remains. I believe that it was this illogical position and the total lack of any flexibility on the part of the Liberals dealing with it which cost them the support of such people as Ludovic Kennedy and Michael Starforth, to name only two Liberals who left that Party later in 1967 and committed themselves to the support of the Scottish National Party.

The two illogicalities which I pointed to in my letter were the contrast between the publicly stated belief of many members of the Liberal Party that it stood for full control by a Scottish Government of the economy and finances of Scotland, and the Liberal Party official line that "Defence would still be controlled from London"; and the claim by Liberals that they stood for Scotland having its own voice and vote in the Common Market when that, obviously, could never be granted if we had anything less than full national status as a self-governing country. I concluded my letter with a classic SNP appeal: "When the Scottish political renaissance has taken us to independence once again, then will be the time to take up left, right or centre views. For the sake of the future of the people of Scotland, I ask you to drop partisan views now. London has divided us to conquer us. Let us not play their game for them when we can only lose."

CHAPTER 7

VICTORY AT HAMILTON, 1967

ONE OF THE MORE remarkable aspects of the growth of the SNP from 1962 to 1968 was its spontaneity. The Party simply did not have the resources to carry out a massive propaganda campaign. As the Party grew, publicity for it kept pace, but this publicity was never massive and was often far from being constructive or helpful to the SNP.

It is not surprising that, as the rate of expansion increased, the national office-bearers, staff and committees became almost swamped. The report of Ian Macdonald, National Organiser, to the 1967 Conference at the beginning of June, contained some figures which give an idea of the expansion.

"In 1966, 113 new branches were recognised compared with 29 in 1965. By 25th April 1967, 63 new branches had been recognised since the beginning of the year compared with 18 in the same period of 1966."

The amount of activity going on cannot be quantified but the burgh, county and district election results reflected that activity. SNP candidates were given over 200,000 votes in the local elections in 1967. There were 27 gains in the burgh elections and 42 in the counties. No seats previously held were lost.

Regretfully, because of personal commitments, I was hardly involved in the local authority elections apart from assisting with producing propaganda in West Lothian in which we fielded over 50 candidates in the six burghs and in the county and district elections. John Hamilton, who had been the sole SNP Councillor for three years in West Lothian County Council, comfortably retained Westfield and Torphichen and we gained seven other seats and as many district council seats as well. In the burghs, we won seats in Bo'ness, Linlithgow, South Queensferry and Whitburn, where one of our candidates, William McBride, topped the poll. The two unsuccessful SNP candidates in Whitburn were not far behind and a Labour candidate was bottom of the poll. In fact, the total SNP vote in Whitburn equalled the total Labour vote—3129 votes each; yet the *West Lothian Courier,* commenting imaginatively on Bill McBride's success in Whitburn, noted that an SNP candidate "actually

96

topped the poll, pushing two very strong Labour members into second and third places, despite the fact that the two remaining SNP candidates ran nowhere in this election." That paper, of course, is nothing if not consistent and invariably writes off any support for the SNP as "protest" or "personality" votes.

This great flood of support was given to a Party about which most of the voters knew very little. With few exceptions, the SNP candidates were totally inexperienced. Their integrity and their willingness to work for the communities in which they lived could hardly be questioned, but the electorate really knew very little about them and some of the candidates unfortunately knew very little about local authority work.

However, the voters must have seen and heard enough of the SNP and had enough faith in Scotland and its people to vote for the SNP. In a few places, of course, the opposition did not recognise its existence, far less its potential threat to traditional voting patterns. In West Lothian, especially in the County Council which the Labour Party had controlled with massive majorities for most of 20 years, the strength of the SNP was identified and attacked with the help of the local press, but elsewhere the SNP usually had the element of surprise on its side.

Well-earned success came in many places, notably in Stirling where the SNP became the largest party and Robert McIntyre was elected Provost. There is no doubt that the tide was running in our direction and we were doing our best to take advantage of it, but we were becoming overwhelmed. I have often said that we needed people who were able to be full-time active politicians. I am sure that we did not gain full advantage from the 1967 - 68 period through lack of leadership skill and time. In 1967, we were being helped by the ineptitude of the Labour Government in their conduct of Scottish affairs. The Tory Party was nowhere in the thoughts of the vast majority of the Scottish people and did not gain from disaffection with Labour as they did in England.

Early in 1967, we again started campaigning strongly against British entry into the Common Market. There were British organisations active in Scotland on the same platform, but it was at this time that we became identified in Scotland as the leading anti-E.E.C. organisation. The subject was being debated in Parliament as the Labour Government at this time were opening negotiations "to enter Europe."

We had an emergency resolution at our National Conference in 1967 re-affirming our opposition to entry without consultation of the Scottish people, and declaring that an independent Scottish Government would not necessarily abide by any agreements made on Scotland's behalf by United Kingdom Governments. In effect this was still "no voice, no entry," although it was couched in more positively critical terms.

After the Conference, we sent a Memorandum to all the States of Europe, through diplomatic channels, advising them of the current political state of Scotland, giving a resumé of the Scottish National Party and its aims, and pointing out that an independent Scottish Parliament would not necessarily feel obliged to honour any agreements made on behalf of the people of Scotland by any British Government. This Memorandum was almost entirely the work of a member of the Economics and Information Department, John Picken, who had previously been employed with the European Parliament Organisation in Strasbourg and who was intensely interested in Foreign Affairs, especially in relation to an independent Scotland. The text of the Memorandum is magnificently formal—John Picken translated it into what I believe was impeccable French.

We are not likely to know the effect of that Memorandum until there are Scottish Embassies in Europe, but I believe that our action, and actions such as the visit of our delegation to the E.E.C. Headquarters in Brussels in February 1970, at least let the English Government know, from unexpected quarters, that the Scottish National Party existed and was active.

The 1967 Conference was the first of the really big SNP Annual Conferences. It had a new air about it. Many new members came as delegates, many of them totally naive about politics but all with a tremendous enthusiasm for the Party and a great faith in the future of Scotland.

Of course, the vast majority of members were in great spirits because of the Pollok by-election result and the Burgh, County and District election results. Winifred Ewing appeared on the Conference platform for the first time, nervous but compelling and giving an indication of the talents she was so soon to exploit in her own campaign. She was elected to National Council and, later, to the National Executive Committee.

A novel feature of the conference compared with previous conferences of the 1960s was the fact that there was a contest for the Chairmanship. Douglas Drysdale had become increasingly restive in the Executive Committee and increasingly critical of Arthur Donaldson's leadership. Douglas Drysdale is a very forthright, honest person who is not afraid to speak his mind but, although he had worked hard for the Party and done a tremendous amount of good work in organisation and finance, he had done little to justify confidence in his political judgment. He had support from a few within the Party, some of whom emerged a few months later as the 1320 Club which may well have had an undercover existence at this time.

On the other hand, Arthur Donaldson's standing was justly very high. His personal abilities, his years of dedication to the Party, his adroitness in the Chair and his wise political counsel and commentary, which appeared for so many years in the columns of the *Scots Independent,* contrasted very favourably in the eyes of the vast majority of delegates with what Douglas Drysdale had to offer. The result was a foregone conclusion, and Arthur Donaldson was elected for an eighth consecutive term of office.

There was one proposed constitutional amendment on the Conference Agenda to which I was strongly opposed. It was a proposal from the Party's Organisation Committee to have the National Executive Committee elected on a representative regional basis, with one person coming from every three or four constituencies in Scotland. I submitted that it would be impossible for anyone to be truly representative in such circumstances and, in any case, such a representative would have no single body to report to.

The West Lothian amendment to which I spoke extended the representative principle by proposing that every constituency in Scotland should send a representative. In fact, what we proposed was a shadow parliament. The Conference accepted our amendment and brought into being the SNP's National Assembly. As the constitutional changes were fundamental, a year was allowed for their introduction, so the Assembly did not meet until June 1968, all the constitutional amendments of the 1967 Conference having become fully operational by the 1968 Conference.

It seemed to some that we did not need this additional national forum but it did a great deal of useful work in the next three years. I believe that the National Party has evolved a democratic and workable constitution which allows for more participation by ordinary members and for more discussion of important political and organisational matters than the constitution of any other political party in Scotland.

The strength of the SNP lies in its branches. In most cases, a branch serves a community, a village or one or two neighbouring villages, a burgh, a ward or even part of a ward.

There are usually several branches in each constituency. Constituency Associations are formed by delegates from the branches and have their own separate office-bearers and funds.

Annual National Conference is the governing body of the Party with delegate representation from every branch, the number of delegates being related to the number of members in the branch; one delegate from each Constituency Association and one delegate from each affiliated organisation. At the time of writing, the affiliated organisations are the Association of Scottish Nationalist Trade Unionists, the Federation of Student Nationalists and the Highlands Area Council.

Between Annual Conferences, the overriding authority of the Party is vested in National Council to which each branch, each Constituency Association and each affiliated organisation may send one delegate. Any number of other members may attend as observers. National Council may deal with any matter at all except certain sections of the Constitution. It meets quarterly and receives reports from the national office-bearers and national committees. It often discusses organisational matters, plans for special campaigns, current affairs of political importance and, less frequently, detailed policy questions.

The National Assembly now consists of two delegates from each constituency, one of whom is the adopted candidate or M.P. This body has mainly been concerned with the detailed discussion and preparation of policy and is becoming increasingly involved in political strategy and in giving overall guidance to the Party and leadership in political matters.

The National Executive Committee consists of 12 National office-bearers elected at the Annual Conference and 10 other elected members, five coming from National Council and five from National Assembly. It meets monthly and deals with the day-to-day running of the Party, politically and organisationally.

This is certainly quite a complex structure but the basis of it is to provide opportunities for discussion, planning and effective action by people who are dedicated to a practical aim and who are prepared to work and sacrifice to achieve it. I do not believe that any alternative arrangement with more authoritarianism and less democracy would be acceptable within the Scottish National Party.

At the time of the 1967 Conference, a senior honours student in Edinburgh University conducted a survey within the Party in order to try to "place the SNP squarely on the map of political ideology." A questionnaire had been carefully designed and a

100

sample of about 50 people was chosen, half of them being national known figures in the Party, mostly from the National Executive Committee, and the other half being members of Edinburgh University Nationalist Club.

The study was based on three hypotheses:

1. That members of the National Executive would show more political experience than Club members.
2. That National Executive members would show a more right-wing tendency than would members of the club.
3. That the sample as a whole would not show any marked tendency to either right or left.

Not surprisingly, hypothesis 1 was clearly proved correct. An interesting finding was that every respondent, in both categories, thought that the SNP would win at least one seat in the next (1970) General Election. Hypothesis 2 was verified at a very low level of significance and could have been explained solely by the age differential. As far as hypothesis 3 was concerned, the scores of both sub-samples were almost identical and both practically dead centre. One of the questions produced quite a surprise result—only three National Executive members thought that Scotland should restrict immigration by "non-British nationals," whereas eight student Club members were prepared to do so.

Such studies are of at least passing interest and usefulness. The vast majority of political observers of the SNP are trying to assess a fresh political and philosophical outlook which has had no counterpart in existing British politics within the experience or understanding of the people designing the surveys and making the observations. It is not what we are that is important to the electorate, it is what they think we are. It is more a question of inspiring confidence than in conforming to some established ideological doctrine. I believe that Winifred Ewing's election five months after our National Conference proves me right.

In the 1967 Hamilton campaign, I was no more than a part-time back room worker helping with policy statements and press material. I was able to do little canvassing, and I spoke at very few meetings, as the demands of my job necessitated much travelling.

The Economics and Information Department took up most of my SNP time. I was very concerned to appoint a Research

Officer, as I sensed the possibility of having an M.P. in the near future. In 1964, when I first really envisaged what election to Westminster would involve, I said that the first person into Parliament would require as "manager and contact in Scotland a person of comparable calibre and understanding who could devote their time all day and every day as a two-way communication link. He or she would have to be in close touch with the M.P. in London, and with the Press and broadcasting authorities in Scotland as a means of communicating with the Scottish people, and regular contact would also be necessary with the Scottish National Party, especially activists concerned with research for propaganda purposes and with active political work."

In August 1967, I persuaded the National Executive Committee to appoint a sub-committee under David Rollo to examine the possibility of appointing a Research Officer. Owing to shortage of funds, it was envisaged at this stage that the appointment would be part-time. The recommendations submitted to the September meeting of the Executive were intended to provide maximum propaganda in quality and quantity for the SNP's campaign leading to and including the next General Election. It was considered necessary to prepare a successor to *SNP and You* dealing mainly with proposals for economic and financial policy and administration in an independent Scotland.

It was expected that, more specifically, the Research Officer would be "studying, collecting, collating, editing and submitting facts and figures on the general economic situation in Scotland, current and potential, with as much emphasis as possible on Finance, Banking and Taxation; Housing; Use of Land and other Natural Resources; Population; Employment and Emigration; Industry; Commerce and Transport; Education and Scientific Research; Defence and Foreign Affairs; Social Services, Industrial Relations, Law, Culture and Recreation."

He would also be "assisting with the drafting of policy proposals in sufficient detail to enable the SNP and its supporters to see clearly how Scotland would become independent, how a Scottish Government would control the financial and economic situation and how Scotland would take her place in the community of nations."

The Executive was willing but there was no suitable person available. Winifred Ewing's election on 2nd November made the matter desperately urgent, so at the November Executive Meeting held on 10th November I volunteered to undertake the

102

appointment as Director of Research. By this stage, the Economics and Information Department, which included many people willing and able to help, was quite effective in discussions and planning, but it was clearly essential to have someone with the time to give direction to the work and to process it, especially now that we had a Member of Parliament whose effectiveness in the fight for self-government would be greatly increased if we could provide her with the best possible research and publicity services.

The Executive was to arrange the terms of the appointment at its December meeting but a road accident on 1st December put me out of the running for this work for at least six months, and no one else was appointed.

When the Economics and Information Department was called to a meeting on 14th October 1967, there were 37 members. Most of them were nationalist politicians with a clear head, good judgment and a desire to help, but few of them had a professional or academic training: they had plenty of ideas but not much knowledge about how to put them into practice. However, several of us had pooled our source material and one of our number, Brian Innes-Will, at this time maintained over 30 files.

For the meeting on 14th October, I submitted a statement of SNP policy proposals on economic matters, with a view to releasing it for publication in order to help in the Hamilton by-election campaign. I believe that the proposals were of great importance for Scotland and the Party. They had evolved from Conference resolutions, research work and discussions within the party over a period of years. The introduction to the statement is as appropriate in 1973 as it was six years ago.

"The basic need in Scotland today is for the people to have faith in themselves and in Scotland and to have the will to make Scotland in the 70s a country of which we shall all be justly proud.

"To generate faith in Scotland among the people requires a sense of security based on two main economic factors:

1. A regular flow of employment opportunities and obvious economic growth.

2. Sufficient housing to reasonable standards.

"To stimulate the will to improve Scotland requires realisation of how much industrial progress has been made in Scotland in recent years, principally as a result of the foresight and efforts of people in Scotland, in spite of having had to suffer unsuitable economic policies pursued by successive government in London. It is also important for the people to realise how much more progress we could make if we really were determined to do so as a nation."

The statement then went on to deal with Transport and with Fuel and Power, two vital factors influencing the economic climate and both under a considerable measure of government control. We referred to the Roads policy which the SNP had published in December 1966, and to the Civil Aviation Policy published a year or two earlier and brought up to date in 1967. Proposals were also made for Docks, Railways and for a Scottish Ministry of Transport. There were detailed proposals based on the SNP's existing Fuel and Power policies.

One of the principal sections dealt with industrial development and opened by quoting from Dr William Robertson, Executive Vice-President of the Scottish Council (Development and Industry): "It is crystal-clear that Scotland must continue to take its own independent initiatives in creating international associations in matters of technology and in broader areas of thought and action. The flood of international events is far too great for Scotland to be able to rely upon London pipelines for its international associations."

The document repeated the belief that we must have an Industrial Development Corporation for industrial regeneration in Scotland. We see the intention in establishing such a corporation as providing the maximum possible professional assistance and capital for economic growth. Industrial research and development must be co-ordinated and management services of all kinds must be provided as well as finance.

There was a section on land use, including the proposals that Scotland should have a six million acre forest by the end of the century, and that, in agriculture, the main aim should be to encourage the maximum production of food in Scotland.

The statement concluded with a section on Banking, Monetary Control and Taxation. "The wealth of Scotland is great, the potential prosperous development of Scotland is great. The SNP is studying proposals for the establishment of a Scottish Government Bank and for the intelligent use of monetary control and a favourable trading position to ensure stability in the Scottish economy."

In the press coverage following the issue of the statement, *The Scotsman* had an interesting paragraph: "It is recalled that the SNP gave notice some years ago that a Scottish Government would stake a claim to gas in the North Sea off the coast of Scotland." In a reference to oil, the statement mentioned in parenthesis "shale and other possible sources." Little did we know how important these "other possible sources" were going to be in only six years' time.

Two days before polling day, I visited Hamilton constituency with two SNP colleagues, Jimmy McGinley and John Miller Gibson. Our canvassing and interviews convinced us that a win was definitely possible. We realised that the Party had fought a very effective campaign. Winifred Ewing had really gone out to meet the people wherever she could find them, round the streets, not only in busy shopping areas, but round the housing schemes as well; she had met and talked with thousands of people throughout the whole constituency. With her vivacious personality, her warm humanity, her intelligence and her debating ability, she projected an image of the party which not another soul in the party could have surpassed.

In the oft-raised question as to whether the electorate votes for parties or for personalities, I come down on the side of those who say that people vote for parties; but people vote for parties as they see them and obviously the better a party is projected, the more votes it will get. Winifred Ewing undoubtedly projected the SNP in a most effective way in Hamilton. It was a team effort and it was well managed. The principal people responsible for running the campaign were her election agent John McAteer, Ian Macdonald who at that time was National Organiser, and Rosemary Hall who was then Organising Secretary. In the last two or three weeks of the campaign, hundreds of people poured into the constituency from all over Scotland to help, and a contingent came up from Wales. The result was of great significance. It was not illogical to have expected it. In politics such things happen, they can be repeated and they can be multiplied. Opponents may talk of "a freak result" or "a flash in the pan" or "by-election fever," but the conditions of the Hamilton by-election were not so exceptional, nor was the state of opinion in Scotland, and I have not the slightest doubt that the future holds other Hamilton-type successes for both Scotland and Wales.

Jimmy McGinley, John Miller Gibson and I had gone back to Hamilton on polling day but we did not wait for the result. We returned home and saw it on television. When the result came over, we hired a taxi and went back to Hamilton to add our congratulations. It was quite an occasion. A hotel near the

SNP's election rooms had been taken over by hundreds of members and supporters and the rejoicing went on there throughout the night. At the centre of it all, like a fairy princess, Winifred Ewing held court. The victory was hers, a just reward for total commitment of her whole personality and all her talents and ability; and that commitment was to continue unabated for more than two and a half years.

The following weeks were absolutely hectic. Rosemary Hall and Ían Macdonald worked night and day with their staffs to cope with floods of enquiries, and people queued in the streets outside our offices to join the Party. The famous train to London was arranged to carry several hundred supporters from all over Scotland who wanted to see Mrs Ewing go to Parliament for the first time. A great crowd of Welshmen also turned up in London on Thursday, 16th November. We had a joint conference with them in the morning, then we all crowded round the public entrance to the House of Commons to await the victor's arrival. Arthur Donaldson and Gwynfor Evans headed the enthusiastic reception committee. A bright red Scottish-built Hillman Imp brought Mrs Ewing to the door. In a few minutes she was in, a lonely figure, fashionably and beautifully dressed, a brilliant jewel amid those drab surroundings.

The public hullabaloo following the election result continued to centre round Winifred Ewing for many months. In the weeks following the victory, the world's press clamoured to interview her, and all Scotland cried out for her to visit them. Her arrival in London was the focal point of the sweeping crescendo of publicity for the Party which reached its peak some six or seven months later. The hundreds of us who had journeyed to Westminster to share in her moment of triumph returned to work on the real source of power, the hearts and minds of the people of Scotland, knowing that at last we had a voice in Parliament which would speak for Scotland's interests first, and not only when they suited the English parties.

The Hamilton result brought a host of new challenges. I tried to keep in daily contact with Mrs Ewing, and I tried to accommodate the news-hungry pressmen. I remember squeezing in a specially arranged pit-head meeting at Polkemmet Colliery for a B.B.C. Panorama programme in which I was interviewed by James Mossman. Polkemmet was well known for the militant attitude of at least a handful of men, many of whom came from Hamilton constituency, so the pit-head meeting was quite lively. After seeing the programme on TV, Oliver Brown told me he had thought such fierce and direct heckling extinct. Perhaps it was in Glasgow, but certainly not in West Lothian.

However, the highlight of the meeting did not appear on TV. I had as my supporter that day Angus McGillveray, one of the staunchest and most forthright Scotsmen I know. When Angus realised I was not convincing some of my audience that *SNP and You* was a reasonably explicit policy document, he stepped forward and announced that he had a copy of the Labour Party's policy in his pocket. He held the audience in suspense with a few choice words before producing a copy of the *Beano*. This received a tremendous reception from the majority of those present. Angus's two minutes were undoubtedly most effective.

On St Andrew's night, I spoke at an SNP public meeting in Castle Douglas, and the next morning, I set off to make calls near Dumfries and Jedburgh and to deliver urgently needed spares to a forestry contractor working near Yetholm. I wanted to reach Edinburgh by 3 p.m. for a meeting of a Heriot-Watt University Committee of which I was convener, but I did not complete my schedule. My van was involved in a crash and my injuries put a curb on activities for several months.

The progress of the Scottish National Party from 1962 - 67 had made the winning of a seat in a by-election almost inevitable. Our leaflet distribution and door-knocking campaign, supplemented by increasing attention from the press, radio and television, resulted in a continuously increasing body of support. However, we suffered, and still suffer, from two handicaps—lack of a daily newspaper, radio or television station with a wholly sympathetic outlook on self-government; and insufficient funds.

During this period, *The Scotsman* and the *Aberdeen Press & Journal* gave our statements and reports fair news coverage and they also gave us the occasional accolade of serious sympathetic consideration in feature articles and editorials. The same two newspapers have continued to give the SNP such coverage. In the *Daily Record,* towards the end of this period, Michael Grieve, writing in a column called "The Voice of Scotland," was also helpful in spreading understanding of and support for the SNP. The *Glasgow Herald* has never, to my knowledge, departed from a Conservative and Unionist attitude to the SNP and at times, particularly after Hamilton, its squeals of criticism rose to falsetto pitch.

An important factor in our success in this period is the fact that the majority of professional politicians and political commentators underestimated the latent desire of the vast majority of the people of Scotland for the establishment of a Scottish Parliament free from English domination.

This ignorance by our political opponents of our sources of power gave us the advantage of surprise until 1968. Although the SNP campaigns in Pollok and in Hamilton had been well covered in the daily press, especially in the closing stages, the English party organisations had not taken us seriously and in any case, at this stage, they did not know how to counter-attack.

In the first two weeks after Winifred Ewing won Hamilton, we probably received as much newspaper coverage as we had been given as a party in the previous 20 years. The same applied to television coverage, and thus began the period of five to six months of the most extensive news coverage the Party had ever experienced. The effect of it was shown in the burgh elections in May 1968, in which we were given more votes than any other party, with nearly 40% of all the votes cast. It was these votes and our sweeping gains in the new burgh of Cumbernauld in June which reinforced the lesson of Hamilton as far as the Tory and Labour Parties were concerned, and thereafter their concerted counter-attacks started in earnest. The effect of their pressure on the news media became apparent later in 1968.

When Mrs Ewing became the M.P. for Hamilton, B.B.C. TV and S.T.V. both had series of weekly parliamentary political programmes. Consequently, she appeared frequently on both channels and, of course, her presence made self-government the number one topic, much to the annoyance, and sometimes fury, of M.P.s of the English parties who took part in programmes with her. After the series ended, they were never repeated. Why? Because the viewers did not want to hear an SNP Member of Parliament? Or because the Establishment did not want them to hear one? The way in which party political broadcasting is manipulated by the English parties to their advantage indicates the way in which their influence altered the shape of all political broadcasting in Scotland after the winter series of 1967 - 68.

A fortnight after the Hamilton result Mrs Ewing started a weekly column in the *Daily Record*. In this column, in her fearless and direct manner, she frequently attacked the hypocrisy of Scottish M.P.s, exposed the inadequacy and duplicity of the Labour Government and pled eloquently for support for self-government for Scotland.

As Michael Grieve's weekly "Voice of Scotland" was also running in the *Record,* it is far from surprising that Labour

M.P.s and other persons in the Labour Party objected very strongly to this continuous stream of SNP propaganda appearing in what the vast majority of Labour supporters and members considered to be virtually their Party newspaper. Nor was it surprising, therefore, that Mrs Ewing's contract was not renewed and Michael Grieve's column eventually disappeared. After Mrs Ewing's election to Parliament, the *Scottish Daily Express* also offered her a weekly column but as she chose to write for the *Record,* she could not write for the *Express.* However, the *Express* did Mrs Ewing and the SNP a service by appointing a member of staff to write a weekly column on "Winnie at Westminster." This must have been just as good value to the SNP in winning support as was the column in the *Record.* This column did not last for long enough to seriously embarrass the Conservative Party, just as the *Record* column ended so as not to prove a similar embarrassment to the Labour Party. However, Mrs Ewing was so active in Parliament in the whole of her two and a half years there that she helped to maintain publicity for the Party at a very much higher level than prior to the Hamilton by-election.

After Mrs Ewing's election to the House of Commons, the writer of an article in the London *Times* said, "Nationalists have to learn that it is the winning of a seat that hurts the big parties, not what they can do or say when they reach the Commons." Basically, that comment is fair and accurate in that it reflects the naked and often unpalatable fact that the currency of political power is in votes, but there is no doubt that Winifred Ewing's active participation in the House of Commons and her writings and speeches as an SNP Member of Parliament gave the affairs of Scotland more prominence than they had received for years, and made some M.P.s very uncomfortable, even if they were not seriously hurt in the process.

As we had expected as a result of an M.P. being elected from our Party, Mrs Ewing's questions produced a flow of interesting and valuable information. Of more political significance were her speeches and her interventions in debates. In the first hectic months, Mrs Ewing must have felt very much on her own. She had the moral and political support of Gwynfor Evans in the House of Commons and the SNP's Economic and Information Department had volunteer helpers, including some in London who helped with questions and motions and facts and figures, but the burden of work she carried herself was immense.

In August of 1968, the Party appointed its first Research

Officer who eased Mrs Ewing's burden considerably. The person appointed was Donald Bain, a graduate of Aberdeen University, who had spent two years on post-graduate work in Canada and had just completed a year of special study at Strathclyde University. His subject was politics, his political sympathies had been with the SNP for several years and his personal qualities were such that he soon proved to be about the best investment the Party had ever made. Now Managing Director of a firm of research consultants in Stirling, his services are still retained by the Party as its Senior Research Consultant.

The other sphere in which our lonely M.P. would have welcomed more professional help right from the beginning was that of publicity, although several journalist friends gave her a lot of help. It was not until the autumn of 1969 that the Party appointed a full-time professional Director of Communications, Douglas Crawford, who gave up the editorship of the magazine *Scotland,* published by the Scottish Council (Development and Industry), to join the staff of the SNP. Like Donald Bain, Douglas Crawford is now in the position of a consultant to the Party, being Managing Director of a Public Relations Company in Edinburgh.

The way in which Winifred Ewing was treated by some of the Scottish M.P.s of the English parties was below the standards of common courtesy which one would expect. The totally deceitful campaign which the Labour Party waged on the subject of Mrs Ewing's attendances is a good example. In fact, her record of attendance and participation was well above the average for an M.P. from Scotland and the interest which she showed in Scottish subjects, reflected in the questions she asked and in the motions she set down, far exceeded the level of interest shown by the other M.P.s from Scotland. Of course the Labour Party had suffered most from the SNP win at Hamilton, and they were determined to discredit the winner. This was another case of lies and gossip to discourage people from voting SNP. As far as service to the constituency is concerned there is no doubt that Winifred Ewing was a great deal more active than her predecessor had been and that she dealt expeditiously and successfully with hundreds of cases and thousands of letters during her two and a half years as Hamilton's M.P.

Winifred Ewing not only led the struggle for self-government during this period, she personified Scotland in a remarkable and powerful way.

CHAPTER 8

STRESS AND STRAIN 1967-68

DURING THE PERIOD in which Mrs Ewing was in the English Parliament, she was a constant reminder to the House of Commons that Scotland, the nation, not merely existed but wanted to *be* a nation again. To many Scots she was "the flower of Scotland" of the popular song. To the representatives of the English Parties in Scotland, she was often like a thistle which they could neither grasp nor crush. They certainly tried. In addition to the personal taunts and provocation and simple rudeness to which some individual M.P.s resorted, the Labour Government and the Tory Opposition had to react officially in order to try to recoup support won from the electorate by the Scottish National Party.

The principal form of reaction by the Government was to set up a Commission under economist Lord Crowther to examine the Constitution of the United Kingdom in order to ascertain whether any changes were necessary. Since the death of Lord Crowther, the Commission has been under the convenership of Lord Kilbrandon, a Scottish Judge known to have respect for the place and rights of Scotland in the U.K. as established by the Act of Union of 1707, since he publicly questioned the legal aspects of entry into the European Common Market as it would affect Scotland.

The appointment of the Commission on the Constitution has been useful from the point of view of the SNP in Scotland and Plaid Cymru in Wales in that it has enabled both Parties to encourage further serious public debate on self-government; but its existence as far as the English Parties are concerned is no more than a device to delay as long as possible the date at which any decision need be taken on Welsh and Scottish self-government. In October 1969, the Party submitted a document of about 6000 words to the Commission and appointed a team of witnesses to give evidence and answer questions. After the Tory Party came to power in the following year, the Commission apparently went into hibernation and, nearly three years later, there is still no sign of any movement.

The Tory reaction to Hamilton and to Mrs Ewing's constant irritations which upset the comfortable control of Scotland from

111

London was the proposal that there should be what they called a "Scottish Assembly." This is well and truly on the shelf, and will remain there until the people of Scotland have the confidence to assert their right to self-government which the SNP evidence to Crowther described as "a moral, political and constitutional issue to be decided by the people of Scotland and not by any commission or other government body."

Another principal reaction of the Labour Government to the rise and support of the Scottish National Party and to the repeated probing and criticising by Winifred Ewing was to set up a Select Committee (*i.e.* a committee of M.P.s) to look into Scottish Affairs. Mrs Ewing was appointed to be a member of the Committee of 16 M.P.s from Scottish constituencies. The work of the Committee consumed a tremendous amount of time and energy. It met over thirty times to hear evidence—for most of a day on twenty-three occasions. It was mainly concerned with enquiry into economic planning by Government in and for Scotland. Never before had Scottish economic affairs been so thoroughly examined and publicised.

Much of the evidence and much of the English Parties' report is deadly dull, and the latter is understandably favourable to the continuation of the system of control under which Scotland has been declining for generations. With the help of Donald Bain, and Dr David Simpson of Stirling University, the SNP's Director of Research at the time, Mrs Ewing prepared and submitted to the Committee a draft report of her own of around 6000 words. This was a *magnum opus* for which Mrs Ewing and her helpers have never received full credit. It was published along with the main report on 13th May 1970, only a day or two before the General Election was announced, so it received practically no publicity. How she coped with this plus all the other things she did, including running a covenant fund-raising scheme for the Party which she started at the end of 1969 and which raised over £6000 for Party Funds in 1970, I simply do not know.

Mrs Ewing's report dealt in detail with the "roots of discontent" in response to which Parliament had set up the Select Committee. As "proof of failure of the present machinery to serve the needs of the Scottish economy," Mrs Ewing compared the economic performance of Scotland with "other North-Western European countries which, like Scotland, suffer the supposed disabilities of small populations, severe climate and remoteness from major markets." The percentage increases of industrial production in 1958 to 1967 were: Finland 88%, Sweden 79%, Denmark 77%, Norway 67% and Scotland 29%." These statistics alone are devastating evidence of the failure of the system in Scotland.

The chronic unemployment rate of Scotland was compared with the situation in other countries with similar effect, but more serious and shocking was the table on the loss or gain from net migration. This was taken from a report by a Working Party on Migration set up in reaction to the Hamilton result, but the report, although printed, was suppressed on the orders of the Secretary of State, William Ross, who refused to answer questions on emigration in Parliament although the findings of the Working Party must have been available to him. The report was "leaked" to the SNP and published in the *Scots Independent* and in *The Scotsman*. When challenged on the suppression of the report at a public meeting in Leith at which Harold Wilson was the main speaker, William Ross was far from pleased. The challenger, Tom Hyde, a well-known SNP member from Edinburgh, was quickly frog-marched out of the hall.

The damning statistics on migration, as set out by the Government's statisticians, show that in 1961 - 66 Scotland was unique among the industrialised and relatively high income countries of Western Europe in experiencing severe net emigration. In fact, in the period Scotland actually *lost* population with a rate of $-100 \cdot 5\%$, although the natural increase by births and the natural decrease by deaths were at normal levels. The Scottish rate was more than twice that of Northern Ireland, Portugal, Greece and Eire, which all had serious problems. The countries one can reasonably compare with Scotland either had increases of population well in excess of the natural increase, *e.g.* England and Wales $+26 \cdot 1\%$, Sweden $+46 \cdot 9\%$; or had insignificant net loss rates, *e.g.* Norway $-3 \cdot 4\%$ and Finland $-9 \cdot 6\%$.

The Scottish National Party had for at least 15 years been trying to draw the attention of the people and their politicians to the extremely serious emigration from Scotland, but it was only in the late 1960s after Winifred Ewing reached the House of Commons that the Scottish representatives of the English Parties even looked at the figures. Labour were in power and they did not like the figures—not because they were serious for Scotland but because their claims to be managing Scottish affairs in the interests of the people of Scotland were shown to be totally fraudulent—so they suppressed them. What kind of morality is that?

In asking Parliamentary questions, Mrs Ewing exposed the fact that in the seventeen years from 1951 *net* loss of population from Scotland totalled over 554,000. The *gross* migration of Scots in the last twenty years must have been around a million—out of a nation of five million. Is it surprising that there is a Scottish National Party? What perhaps *is* incredible is the apathy with which the publication of such figures is received—but of course the SNP has had no chance of publicising such matters in a dramatic way such as in a documentary TV programme.

In his book *Facts and Comparisons*, Donald Bain deals in detail with emigration, showing the very serious effects it has had on the population structure—the working population is going down and the proportion of elderly folk is going up. He also draws attention to the "collossal loss in terms of investment. For example, it has been estimated that the cost of educating a child amounts to £3000; thus in terms of loss in basic educational investment, a net outflow of 40,000 people is equivalent to a loss of £120 million per year—and this does not take into account other forms of investment such as health and welfare facilities, family allowances, university and technical education, teacher training etc. In sheer financial terms, emigration represents a drain down which a very large part of Scotland's potential wealth is disappearing."

The foregoing references show how invaluable Winifred Ewing's two and a half years in Parliament have been and will continue to be for the future of Scotland. Looking back and considering what she did in her total commitment of her time, her intellectual ability and resources and her emotions, I feel somewhat bitter that many people of Hamilton had their minds poisoned against such a brilliant M.P.; and I realise that the Scottish National Party hardly deserved her sacrifices. While she was battling on her own against the combined forces of the English Parties and the might of Government, many so called stalwarts of Scotland were criticising her over their evening pints.

The Party did not grow without stresses and strains resulting from tension between persons of different ideologies whose meeting ground was self-government for Scotland. The majority of members support the view that the SNP should prepare policies as the achievement of self-government implies that the SNP may be called upon to take part in forming a government. The belief that this may happen is entirely a practical one, based on the democratic principle which is the foundation of the SNP's

114

existence—that the people of Scotland will only get self-government by voting for it—and the fact that the SNP is the only party presently seeking a mandate for self-government.

At the time when self-government is won, one of the principal assumptions is that the Scottish National Party will have the allegiance of the majority of the Members of Parliament, and will enjoy the confidence of more of the voters of Scotland than any other party. That confidence will not be based only on belief in self-government as a principle. It will also be based on belief that the candidates of the Scottish National Party are capable of undertaking the running of Scottish affairs within a Scottish Parliament.

It follows, therefore, that the Scottish National Party must prepare for such an eventuality, and preparation includes drafting of policies which can be put before the electorate as proof of good faith and understanding of what is required in Scotland.

One of the qualities of the SNP is that when such policies are debated, hammered out and supported by a majority, they are invariably accepted without question and in good grace by the liberal minded and socialist members of the Party whether they are particularly "left wing" policies or not, whereas other elements in the Party are often critical and unwilling to accept democratically formulated policies. Such discomfort in the face of democracy can cause restlessness. In my experience, many of our internal political troubles in the Party have resulted from a form of elitism favoured by a very small number of such people.

As I have already remarked, I suspect that the 1320 Club was in existence at the time of our Annual Conference in 1967. In the autumn of that year, while the Hamilton election campaign was under way, the National Executive was asked by Dr George Philp of Glasgow to give a ruling as to whether or not he could join a new club called the 1320 Club. Dr Philp had joined the SNP in the spring of 1966 and, although very few knew him, had found himself elected to the National Executive Committee in the summer of that year. However, he did not stand for re-election in 1967. This experience lay behind the introduction in 1967 of a rule requiring nominees for N.E.C. to have been in the Party for at least one year.

Several of us who could see a divisive confrontation in the offing tried to persuade Dr Philp not to proceed with his demand that the Executive give a ruling. However, he was not persuaded. The ruling, after examination of the constitution of the 1320 Club which Dr Philp submitted, was that membership of the

Club was incompatible with membership of the SNP. Because of the provisions of our own constitution, the N.E.C. had to place the matter before the whole party in National Council at its next meeting which was in March 1968.

Naturally, there was quite a buzz in the Party and in the national press when the agenda for National Council went out in February 1968 with a resolution from the Executive proposing that membership of the 1320 Club and membership of the SNP should be made incompatible. The euphoria of Hamilton was still very much in the air at this time, and to many new members it must have seemed extraordinary for the Party to be considering such a resolution, especially as the patron of the Club was that very distinguished Scot, Lord John Boyd-Orr, who, I am certain, was only a figure-head and took no part in the running of the Club.

Arthur Donaldson expressed the feelings of the Executive by saying: "We won't allow a group to form themselves into a secret pressure group within the Scottish National Party, and that is what the 1320 Club are trying to do. Membership of the 1320 Club is only by invitation and one of the clauses in the enrolment form demands that the membership of the Club be kept secret, even to other members." In fact, the 1320 Club constitution at the time ruled that the Club Executive was solely responsible for the choosing of members. The Club refused to consider a change before the SNP National Council meeting, but I believe they changed this later.

Some people tried to keep the argument on principles only but, as I wrote at the time in the *Scots Independent,* "We are not dealing with an abstract proposition but with facts and with people and with their statements and known attitudes and these must be considered along with the principles."

I warned that "If the SNP's party discipline appears to the world at large to allow uncontrolled propagation of the ideas of dictatorial non-elected government and the establishment now of a "Scottish Liberation Army," then the world at large may be justified in doubting the sincerity of the declared democratic and non-violent aims and methods of the S.N.P. and in doubting the Party's ability to effectively control those in its membership who are in favour of direct action and dictatorship. Freedom of speech within the Party is not in question but if those people, who favour aims and methods which the Party does not accept, and who seek or have sought or have been proposed for positions of authority in the Party without success, set up another

116

organisation ostensibly to help the Party but embodying the objectionable aims and methods, then the Party has a duty to examine that organisation."

Council voted by a large majority in support of the Executive resolution. I had not the slightest doubt then nor have I had any doubts since that the Party made the right decision. No political party founded on belief in democracy could have taken any course other than that taken by the SNP in March 1968. The question of incompatibility has been raised at National Council on several occasions since, but the Party has maintained the status quo established in March 1968.

The Annual Conference of 1968 reflected a desire to give leadership in the very new situation in which the Party found itself. The victory at Hamilton and the sweeping successes in the Burgh Elections gave many the impression that Independence was just a few months away. There was no serious talk in such terms among the experienced members of the Party. The most optimistic forecast within our ranks was reflected in a slogan, "Scotland Free by '73." There were many of us, however, who considered that far too optimistic in spite of the successes of the previous six months.

Nevertheless, our attention was focussed as never before on the need to make preparations for the real possibility, in the foreseeable future, of having to face the responsibility of negotiating with the English Government. The Party's concentration on such matters was a reflection of the many relevant questions asked by members of the public, by our opponents, and by journalists and other writers and commentators.

It is not surprising to find, therefore, that the first resolutions on the Conference Agenda all dealt with weighty financial and economic matters such as accepting a fair share of the U.K. national debt, the establishment of a Scottish Central Bank, the shaping of financial policies to achieve full employment, and the assurance that the Scottish Government would safeguard the rights of citizens of Scotland entitled to pensions from a British Government source.

These resolutions were the work of the Economics and Information Committee in general, and a sub-committee on Finance and Taxation in particular led by Mr William Martin of Glasgow, who was mainly responsible for stimulating widespread discussion throughout the Party on finance. For many years, the Party had advocated that governments should make loans to public authorities at very low rates of interest or even interest free. Mr Martin re-awakened interest in the principle and ran two very successful one-day conferences on monetary affairs a few weeks before Annual Conference.

In speaking on the resolution on the national debt, I said, "We must always have as the basis of our thoughts the fact that we seek to act on behalf of the people of Scotland. Their rights and interests must be paramount in our deliberations. The growing support that we have from the people of Scotland is a trust that we must respect. Ours is a full cup. Let us be strong and steady in holding it. Let it not be spilled.

"It is an act of faith in themselves for the people of Scotland to entrust their future to the SNP, and we are nothing if we are not seeking in the very first instance to be true to that faith. We must be honest with ourselves and, in the matter of this resolution and all it implies, we must be true to the interests and rights of all the people of Scotland."

I called the resolution a "declaration of intent" which had four points to be considered. We had to make our intentions clear, yet we were to avoid manufacturing potential difficulties for our representatives in negotiation. We would be seeking an honourable settlement, pointing out our entitlement not only to claim our share of the assets of the British Government but to bring into account all the effects of generations of mis-government and neglect, such as the disproportionate war sacrifices, the cost of forced emigration, the wasteful miseries of unemployment, the greedy exploitation of some of our resources and the neglect of others and, of course, the result of years of discrimination in Government spending in favour of England.

The third point was to assert that we would honour debts and obligations which we undertook to fulfil. "By our integrity shall we be known," I said. "We must establish and consolidate our moral credit as well as our financial credit in world circles."

The fourth point I made was connected with a new aspect of the Party constitution. The National Assembly which we agreed to have in 1967 was just about to come into operation, following our 1968 Conference. In a reference to negotiations at Westminster in general, and financial negotiations in particular, I said, "The SNP representatives will not be people at a distance, remote from us. We seek a fraternal society, not a protective paternalism. Our Party's new National Assembly will provide a truly democratic forum with a continual constructive dialogue between our representatives in Westminster and the people of Scotland. We aim to establish the best possible form of social, economic and political democracy in Scotland and one of the main public starting points of this development will be in our negotiations with Whitehall. This Resolution provides guidelines for the Party and for its representatives."

Not surprisingly, in the circumstances, I made reference to "our opening skirmishes in Westminster after an unwelcome space of 22 years. The people of Hamilton have opened up the parliamentary channels for the voice of the people of Scotland. Mrs Ewing is doing all she possibly can to ensure that these channels will never be closed again." In concluding, I said, "We will not put up with stalling. We will not haggle about the last half million to delay agreement on the date of Independence. We want to get on with the job of making Scotland a country to be proud of. This resolution is fair and reasonable. It shows our willingness to be fair and reasonable, provided the British Government is fair and reasonable. It shows the world at large that we seek a place of integrity in international trade and finance and it shows that we have a realistic view about the economic future of Scotland." Conference passed the resolution overwhelmingly.

The Conference gave a tremendous reception to Mrs Ewing. She had worked seven days a week non-stop since her election six months earlier, reflecting not only a conscientious respect for duty but a robust constitution. Publications Department produced in time for the Conference *Scotland Versus Whitehall—Winifred Ewing's Black Book*, which contained a telling selection of parliamentary questions and answers providing a wealth of previously undisclosed information about the state of Scotland. For example, in extracting from this booklet the figures from answers on only five subjects—cost of educating emigrants, defence contracts, expenditure by the Ministry of Technology, income tax relief on housing mortgage interest, and selective employment tax figures—one can reach an annual value of £142 million which one can justifiably claim to be a subsidy of England. This figure completely offsets the claim by the English parties, also published in the *Black Book,* that, on what the Treasury fondly calls "Identifiable Expenditure," Scotland was subsidised by England.

Such figures generally confuse most people, and because the Treasury sits on some of the facts and the ministers responsible can invariably find evasive answers if they do not want to disclose facts or cannot do so, and because the Opposition and the Government, no matter which English Party is in power, are in total agreement with each other as far as regarding the cause of the SNP is concerned, it is almost impossible to compile a full and accurate statement of the situation.

However, Mrs Ewing and her questions yielded a mine of information, much of which was used in the compilation of *Scotland—Facts and Comparisons,* the ultimate product of all our effort over the years to produce a Candidate's Handbook.

Two other resolutions of importance for the future were dealt with in Aberdeen in 1968. One was submitted by Arthur Donaldson as convener of the Party's committee on a Scottish Constitution. In introducing it he said, "On the need for a written constitution there seems to be no substantial adverse opinion. This is probably explained by the unsatisfactory experience we have had with the unwritten constitution of the United Kingdom."

Mr Donaldson recalled that the Party at previous Annual Conferences had already taken a number of important decisions relative to a constitution, mainly concerned with national and individual rights and liberties. Some examples were:

"Scotland's national sovereignty is equal to that of any other state and may be qualified only by agreements freely entered into with other nations in order to further international co-operation and world peace. These agreements and qualifications must be terminable by the National Assembly and provisions to that effect will be inserted in all such agreements.

"Freedom of conscience and the free confession and practice of religion are guaranteed to every citizen. The state shall not discriminate on grounds of race, religion, personal beliefs or status.

"The land and all natural resources in Scotland belong to the people and shall be held subject to the constitution and the control of the National Assembly.

"The right to form and operate trade unions and trade associations is absolute but subject to legislative control by the National Assembly.

"The right to own private property is challengeable only by due process of law and with fair compensation and then only where the needs of the community clearly require precedence over the rights of the individual.

"Access to hills and mountains is guaranteed where there is no serious interference with agriculture or forestry.

"In Gaelic-speaking areas, the Gaelic language will have equal status with English."

Since the 1968 Conference, our constitutional proposals have been augmented by further decisions, for example, that the National Assembly will consist of one chamber of 200 members, and that a single transferable voting system will be used in all elections.

The other resolution with a long-term effect was one setting out the principles of a policy on defence. The resolution aroused tremendous interest and there were nine amendments on the agenda. It was mainly a re-statement of existing Party policy. It confirmed that "the primary responsibility for the defence of Scotland must rest on the Government and citizens of Scotland; that the Government shall hold available such forces as may be required to honour Scotland's obligations to the United Nations Organisation; that the Government shall not permit the existence of foreign bases on Scottish soil or on Scottish waters; and shall become a signatory to the Treaty to limit the spread of nuclear weapons"; and a suggested limit on government expenditure on defence was accepted, at a level comparable with defence expenditure levels in the smaller states of Europe.

That resolution was the last on the Conference agenda and thus ended the conference which marked a peak in the Party's fortunes. Had there been another by-election in Scotland within a year of Hamilton, it seems more than likely that, wherever situated, the constituency would have been won for the Scottish National Party. Such a result would have doubled our strength in the House of Commons and provided someone to share the huge burden carried by Mrs Ewing. It would also have reinforced the credibility established by the Hamilton result, but we were not to have the chance of a by-election for more than a year.

With the benefit of hindsight, it is possible to see the important factors which affected the Party's fortunes from mid-1968 onwards. One was political inexperience, and this made us particularly vulnerable to attack by experienced opponents in the town councils, especially in the cities. In Aberdeen and particularly in Dundee, our sole representatives had a tough time. They both carried the flag with honour—Alex MacDonald in Aberdeen and Tom McFetteridge in Dundee. There was a "balance of power situation" in Dundee with Councillor McFefteridge effectively holding a casting vote, so he was in a most unenviable situation in a city not unknown for the robust nature of its politics. Councillor McFetteridge was fearless in exposing various malpractices, and he and his family paid for his patriotism and honesty, suffering persecution, worry and ill-health. Unfortunately, the Party's organisation in Dundee was insufficiently united to give him the moral and political support which he deserved.

Tom McFetteridge had been a member of the Party for twenty years and he was fully conversant with the Party's outlook and democratic structure so, as well as being our heavily-worked sole councillor, he was one of the Party's "anchormen" inside the Party organisation. Membership had grown and it included a number of budding politicians who were more concerned with keeping themselves in positions of power in the Party than anything else. Some were able speakers and organisers and the resulting ructions did not help Councillor McFetteridge or the Party. This intrigue and thrusting for power dominated and decimated the Party in Dundee. Not surprisingly some of the troubles splashed into the Dundee papers with a consequent ill effect on our campaign for self-government in that city. However, the passage of time and a firm line from the Executive eventually dispersed the disruptive elements, leaving a well-functioning Branch in Broughty Ferry. It was this Branch which provided much of the manpower and leadership for the 1973 by-election campaign of Gordon Wilson.

In Edinburgh, our councillors had, collectively, very little knowledge of, or experience in the Party and none at all in local authority work. They lacked leadership and guidance not only among themselves but from the Party's Edinburgh Regional Council. The situation in Edinburgh was a clear case of massive support being given by a public eager for improvement and reform to a party which did not have the strength of organisation or experience to withstand the attacks of the Establishment parties, who will gladly forget their differences of left and right to combine against Scotland's National Party.

In Glasgow, our 13 councillors made a tremendous and brave effort under the leadership of George Leslie. In this group, we had brains, ability and dedication. The self-sacrifice involved was tremendous, mainly because of the need to spend several hours of practically every day of the week on Council work if one was conscientious—and the SNP members were conscientious.

They really had worked hard planning the improvement of Glasgow's administration and they had some excellent ideas, but the Establishment Councillors, both Labour and Tory (including the Progressives under the Tory label) were far too concerned about keeping power to themselves to bother about the SNP

Councillors except to make sure that they were hammered into the ground. In the 1968 Election Labour had lost control of Glasgow after many years of domination, so they had no ear for the SNP Councillors who had apparently brought about their defeat. They were concerned with avenging that defeat by doing all in their power to discredit the Scottish National Party. The Tories were equally hard on the SNP because we were seen as an obstacle which prevented them retaining the power they so precariously held.

Our Councillors have been criticised within the Party for "not sticking to an SNP line," but when there is a yes/no vote being taken with the Labour Party on one side and the Tory Party on the other, responsibility demands that conscientious councillors vote one way or the other. In fact, in the first year in which the 13 SNP Councillors were on Glasgow Town Council, Labour and Tory combined against the SNP more often than SNP combined with either against the other.

In an article in the *Scots Independent* of March 1972, George Leslie lists the achievements of the SNP on Glasgow Town Council. In fact, they achieved more of *their* 1968 manifesto than the Tories achieved in theirs. George Leslie's analysis of the rejection of 1971 seems sense to me.

He wrote: "Those who voted for us in 1968 did not expect us to be good councillors. The SNP represented a fresh organisation untainted by the shabby corruption that dominated Glasgow's political set-up. What the electors wanted was not councillors who would quickly gain experience and mark-up a small achievement here or there. What was wanted was an action group to take an explosive stand of non-co-operation with the two-party dictatorship."

Clearly, as George Leslie said, such a stance is difficult and would require councillors experienced in this type of conflict. It would also require outside support even in the face of unwelcome publicity, and this was not forthcoming, mainly, I believe, because most of our Party leaders in Glasgow were on the Council and so involved with Council work that the organisational work and fund-raising and general Party morale in the city suffered from lack of leadership. As George Leslie concluded, "We were not ready, but for Scotland's sake, let us be ready next time. We must recognise that the opposition will stop at nothing to squash our fight for freedom as they accelerate the anglicisation of Scotland. Success rewards only those who are prepared and who are determined not to fail."

123

We have certainly gained in experience since 1968. Although the total membership of the Party today is less than it was then, the more significant figures of experienced local authority councillors, Parliamentary candidates, organisers and activists committed to regular work on behalf of the Party at Branch, constituency, regional and national levels are undoubtedly much larger than they were in 1968. In the important field of public relations, we are much better equipped to cope with the situation than before. This was particularly evident in the Dundee by-election campaign of March 1973. It was extremely hard-fought by the Tory and Labour Parties, as well as by the SNP, and the Liberals no doubt did their best. The Party's maturity and ability to cope with the public relations of the campaign as well as with the work of canvassing and distributing propaganda, are reflected in the result and in the very high morale of the Party members in Dundee following the result.

In 1968 - 69, the *Glasgow Herald* frequently attacked the SNP, often singling out George Leslie in particular for criticism. One of the subjects with which it tried to discredit us in Conservative eyes, by trying to brand us as revolutionary socialists, was the formation of a society to commemorate one of the greatest working-class leaders Scotland has ever seen —John MacLean, who, in his call for the formation of a Scottish socialist republic, declared his belief in self-government for the people of Scotland as well as his belief in socialism. In his time, he was rejected by the Labour Party and spurned by the Communist Party. He was hounded by the British Government and imprisoned because of his opposition to war. He was a saintly, dedicated, non-violent man whose self-sacrifice for the people of Scotland should be an example to Scots of all political creeds.

That was certainly the light in which I am sure he was seen by the majority of those who agreed to support the foundation of a society to commemorate him. Along with George Leslie, I, and other members of the Party, gave the project my support, as did The Very Reverend Dr George Macleod, M.C., a former Moderator of the General Assembly of the Church of Scotland, and Mr John Johnston, Lord Provost of the City of Glasgow. These men were not attacked for their commitment to support commemoration of John MacLean. Neither was I, although, from the national political point of view, I was in a similar position to George Leslie as we were both Vice-Chairmen of the SNP. One cannot help thinking of his position as our prospective candidate for Pollok constituency, represented at the time, on a minority vote, by the Tory Party in the person of Professor Esmond Wright, who was a Director of the firm publishing the *Glasgow Herald.*

Members of the English Establishment, who have influence with the media, are often in a position to affect what we see and hear in Scotland. Can they all say, as John MacLean said, "I have squared my conscience with my intellect"?

Another factor related to the foregoing points concerning lack of experience and unprincipled and continuous attacks on the Party was the fact that, as with any movement in a similar position, the first flush of public enthusiasm had brought us quite a large number of fair weather recruits, who knew very little about the Party's aims, philosophy, policy and constitution, and who had no more than superficial knowledge of what was required of leadership at any level. There is no doubt that we received a considerable amount of emotional commitment from people who expected us to work miracles overnight because they recognised in what they saw of us a rather exciting radical Party, in fact the only radical Party in Scotland. We were then, and still are, willing to discuss quite openly with anybody at any time any matter of consequence affecting the interests of the people of Scotland. We appealed to many people because we were prepared to listen to them and to talk in their language. We helped them to feel a little less lonely in their individual struggles to overcome their own particular problems; so they voted for us.

After May 1968, a great many of our leading activists were so fully committed as local authority councillors or in dealing with the fundamental organisational work of preparation for the General Election, that we lost from our canvassing teams a large number of people who had carried out the dialogue with the electorate. Instead of continuing open discussion with people on the need for self-government and for reform in so much of Scotland's social and economic life, we had to spend a great deal of thought and energy on countering the avalanche of attacks now being made on us not only from parliamentary level via press, television, radio and meetings, but also through city, town and county councils, trades councils, trade union meetings, pubs, clubs and every other place where people gather and talk.

Being put on the defensive when you believe implicitly that you are standing for truth and the good of your country, especially when you are being attacked by people who have the whole weight of Government and Opposition and a very big share of the media behind them, is a salutary experience. Thus it was with the Scottish National Party. However, it hardened and trained thousands of us throughout Scotland, and we are much better equipped to cope with the wave of support which is currently flowing towards us.

In several local authorities, the Party has had the converse experience of being in a position of power. The large burghs of Stirling and Cumbernauld are the prime examples. In Stirling, the SNP has not held overall control, but as the largest party in the Council since 1967 it has, under Robert McIntyre's leadership as Provost, retained the confidence of a substantial proportion of the electorate. In Cumbernauld, the Party has held a position of overall control, with a clear majority since the Burgh was established in 1968. Throughout these years the skilful management of Provost Gordon Murray and his fellow Councillors has held the support of a majority of the voters. The example of the Party representatives in these Burghs, and in other authorities in which SNP Councillors have had the continued support and respect of the communities they serve, has been a source of encouragement throughout the Party, especially in places where our 1968 support has declined under pressure from the English Parties.

126

CHAPTER 9

A PARTY MATURES, 1969-70

THE PRESSURES on the more experienced active members of the Party increased tremendously in 1968 and 1969. There was the clamour for leadership by the vast army of new members who had little appreciation of the long hard fight which the Party had made and still had to make to achieve self-government. They also had little appreciation of the Party's slender resources. The only person able to give full-time political leadership was Winifred Ewing and she was tremendously overworked. It was as if she had been thrust into top gear with no opportunity for slowing down. She was expected to speak with knowledge and conviction on any subject of the day from agricultural subsidies to the prospects of the electronics industry; she could not stand aside from debates on such subjects as the war in Biafra and British support of the United States in Vietnam; she received a regular flow of letters and suggestions, many from cranks; she was expected to attend the National Executive Committee and National Council of the Party and to speak in every constituency in Scotland, and she had her own constituency to look after as a working M.P. Her life must have been hell at this stage and few in the Party appreciated it, partly because of her intense loyalty and her ability to give a lead no matter how she felt, and partly because most of those who could have helped were under severe pressures themselves, with a living to earn and with heavy responsibilities within the Party.

As well as trying to cope with the new members and the setting up of organisation and the training of people for the coming General Election Campaign, we now had many local authority councillors, and their positions of responsibility gave the English Parties more scope to attack us. Their activists were quite accustomed to the political dog-fight of right versus left, whereas many of our exposed activists in councils or in positions of leadership in branches or constituencies were inexperienced and naive. It is not surprising that our image was not maintained by the press.

The Party's structure was changing, and not before time. The accumulation of work undertaken by the National Executive

Committee in 1967 - 68 had been almost intolerable. The need for a larger staff at H.Q. had become obvious, so additional clerical staff was engaged. The National Assembly (called National Executive Assembly at this period) took over from the Executive Committee the work of directing and controlling policy making and this made a tremendous difference, but concentration on dealing with policies took up the time and energies of many people who would otherwise have been engaged on canvassing and organisation.

Douglas Henderson, as Director of Internal Training, with a team of volunteer helpers, ran courses on various aspects of electioneering throughout the country. This work undoubtedly proved to be of great value in the 1970 General Election.

Naturally, everyone in the Party felt the strain of these pressures in 1968. The most serious were totally outwith the control of the Party—those resulting from the hostility of the English parties in Scotland to the SNP in general and particularly to Mrs Ewing. Nevertheless, as 1968 drew to a close, it was obvious that a large number of members within the Party believed that some internal changes were necessary to combat more successfully the forces ranged against us. The Party generally began to look critically at the leadership and, towards the end of the year, I was asked by several people in different parts of Scotland if I would allow myself to be nominated as a candidate for the chairmanship of the Party, in the elections to be held at the Annual Conference in Oban in May 1969.

In previous years, on receipt of nominations for the post of Chairman, my decision not to stand had been made immediately, without any doubts in my mind. I had been involved intimately enough for long enough in the work of the Party to have some appreciation of the responsibilities of the Chair; I did not really want them, and I did not want to oppose Arthur Donaldson. In all the fundamentals of our philosophy and outlook, our aims and policies and attitudes to the structure and operation of the Party, we were in complete agreement. Where we had disagreed in Executive meetings it was disagreement between experience and inexperience in almost every case. In many ways, we had undertaken a similar kind of work in the Party. In the 1940s Arthur Donaldson had been greatly involved in the work of evolving cohesive policy for an independent Scotland, and I had played a similar rôle in the 1960s.

When Mr Donaldson knew that I was willing to accept nomination and stand for election as Chairman, he decided not to stand. He did not in any way endorse my nomination. However, the widespread apprehension and dismay with which his announcement was greeted resulted in him being asked by a large number of active members and branches to reconsider his decision which, in the event, he did. We both stood because we felt it was our duty to stand. Other people who had been nominated withdrew before circulation of the final agenda, and at the Conference it was a "straight fight."

There was no campaigning and if any lobbying was done, I was not aware of it. Both Arthur Donaldson and myself were prepared with equanimity to accept the decision of the Party. It happened to be for me, but there was neither jealousy nor acrimony and Mr Donaldson continued to be a member of the National Executive Committee.

Being apprehensive about the rather shrill cries at the Conference for the blood of the Establishment who were constantly attacking us, I counselled a more restrained line than some other speakers, saying: "We have got to distinguish between the opponent and the misguided and the uncommitted, because the misguided and the uncommitted are potential delegates at this Conference. Those people are the people of Scotland whom we seek to represent; they are not altogether against us. In our attacks we must be careful to avoid hitting those whom we want to bring to our side. There are people we have got to hit and hit hard, those who try to prevent the evolution of true democracy in Scotland. Our propaganda, while it must hit hard, must speak the truth and must never degenerate into the low kind of thing which is used against us."

Conflict between my approach and a more wholesale destructive approach was apparent for a considerable time in the Executive Committee because I disagreed with Michael Grieve on the subject. It was a question of degree. Michael is such a wholly committed and uncompromising kind of person, like his father, Hugh MacDiarmid, that my opposition was always tempered by admiration. Many in the Party agreed with Michael Grieve's approach. He scripted our annual five minutes on TV in 1970, for Sam Purdie to project. Sam spent 4 minutes 40 seconds attacking the Labour Party. Within the SNP there were immediate cries of "hurrah" and as many immediate cries of pain. Letters poured into H.Q. and to the *Scots Independent* from both sides. The majority was conclusively for moderation when the matter was debated at National Council.

Earlier in 1970, Michael Grieve, assisted by Donald Bain,

had scripted my five minutes on TV in the General Election allocation. I was pleased with the script written for me and there was lots of favourable reaction and no criticism. I once had a plumber in the house who said, "Hot water is funny stuff." So is publicity. If you know what you want, it will serve you well, but you must get the direction of flow and the temperature right.

Looking back, one can see that the Party's Annual Conference in Aberdeen in 1968 marked the highest point reached in the wave of support for self-government which had been steadily growing in the previous seven years. From mid-1968 onwards, the greatly expanded and enthusiastic membership was exposed to serious and continuous counter-attack, a new phenomenon reflecting the progress of the SNP. The 1969 Conference in Oban showed the disappointment and frustration of some who were upset by these counter-attacks. Many new members had not fully realised the enormity of the task the Scottish National Party had undertaken with such slender resources in comparison with the wealth and entrenched powers of the political parties of the English Establishment. There were also other reasons for recalling that conference. It was the first conference at which detailed policies had been brought from the National Assembly. As some delegates were more enthusiastic than experienced, and as some of the policies were too detailed and had not been thought out fully, one or two of the debates were difficult to control, and in reporting these the press representatives had a field day. However, some of them recognised that in the Scottish National Party, democracy meant something. The correspondent of *The Economist* wrote, "The fact is that the SNP runs its affairs so democratically that other party managers would die of the collywobbles. There may be both a lack of SNP policy and a lack of policy definition but the SNP is also facing popular insistence on detailed assessments in all they say and do that is never put to Tory or Labour politicians."

There was one asset which we had which other Parties have envied. We had a weekly newspaper of our own, the *Scots Independent*. This paper is not owned or controlled by the Party but it has always been totally identified with the Party. It was founded in 1928 and has continued uninterrupted publication ever since, sometimes as a monthly and sometimes as a weekly. Throughout the whole of the 1960s it was published every week. From the beginning of 1968, it was edited by Michael Grieve, one of the best and most pungent feature writers in Scotland.

The *Scots Independent* has always been a political paper and as such it has never had a wide appeal, but it has been invaluable in educating the SNP membership, in encouraging its readers to continue the fight for self-government, and as a valuable channel of communication within the Party. It was unfortunate that the almost inevitable financial stringency which resulted from the decline in the Party's fortunes made it necessary for Michael Grieve to be dropped as Editor towards the end of 1969. If he can be faulted for his editorship, it would be on the grounds that he wrote too much of the paper himself in his aggressive style; but anyone who has tried knows how tremendously difficult it is to get people to write articles for nothing and deliver them on time ready for publication. Of the great extent of his dedication and self-sacrifice, there is no question.

Two stalwart nationalists who have contributed much to the paper, and still do, are the cartoonists Ewen Bain and Mally McCormick. The *Scots Independent* and the SNP are indeed most fortunate to have the help of these two talented men, who, with Oliver Brown in his regular commentaries, bring wit and humour which are essential for our sense of proportion and maturity. The invisible men behind the scenes who have regularly seen the paper through the press and dealt on an entirely voluntary basis with all the managerial and accounting problems are Tom Preston, a banker in Airdrie, and Archie Young, Manager of the Technical Services Organisation in Stirling University. Murdo Young has been the paper's "factotum" for many, many years, unselfishly giving really reliable service to the cause. There are also the sellers of the *Scots Independent*. Some individual members have sold dozens every week for years on end. With this kind of devotion, which is to be found all over Scotland, our cause will not be lost.

The debate within the Party as to whether we should have "policies" or not has gone on to a greater or lesser extent since the Party was founded. Readers of this book will realise that I am in favour of the Party examining the fabric of life in Scotland and drafting policies with a view to making proposals for improving that fabric, not only when we have self-government but also in the current political context. It seems to me to be much more important to do that than to fail to do so simply to avoid getting caught up in "right versus left" argument.

Writing in the *Scots Independent* in February 1969, I said: "No other party has undertaken to anything like the same extent the task the SNP has undertaken in preparing policies for an independent Scotland. We have a tremendous responsibility to Scotland in this respect and that is why the framing of policy resolutions for the Annual Conference of 1969 is of such importance.

"We already have the guidance of many years of policy-making on broad lines, and of a few years of policy-making in more detail, but the past six months must surely have seen activity in these spheres on a scale never known in Scotland before, because the twenty-two policy committees of the National Assembly, involving several hundred people, have been working against the clock, gathering information, opinion and advice to establish bases for their drafts and proposals.

"Not only the policy committees, however, are working against the clock—the whole Party is doing that. Years ago, the sense of urgency for the regaining of Scottish independence was held by only a few people. Their cries were largely unheeded until recent years. Today there are far more people seeking the return of self-government to Scotland than ever before. Those of us who are active in the ranks of the Party today must keep reminding ourselves and our neighbours that time is not on our side."

The essence of the matter then and now is "Scottish solutions for Scottish problems." It is quite clear that if the Scottish people do not assert their right to independence, there will be no such thing as a Scottish problem in the course of a generation or so, because we will be assimilated by England and what are now Scottish problems will be English regional problems—which is the present way in which most people outside of Scotland see Scottish problems. The function of our National Assembly in producing policies is based on our declared intention to put the interests of the Scottish people first, and among these interests we have a responsibility, almost above all other responsibilities, to cherish the humanitarian and cultural heritage of the Scots, which should naturally underlie any policies whether they are dealing with economics or social or cultural matters.

Consisting largely of radically-minded people, the Scottish National Party has been evolving an outlook and a philosophy which goes much deeper than a simple rejection of the English Parties in Scotland; but there are obvious difficulties in projecting ourselves as a radical reforming party as well as an independence party. The greatest single difficulty is lack of television time and newspaper coverage for our views. Philosophy and policies

132

based on reason and logic have little news value, but they *could* be the subject of current affairs discussions in print and on the air, especially when they relate to the present and to the immediate future. As Lord Beveridge said of broadcasting arrangements, "Minorities have the right to become majorities." Most of the controllers of broadcasting and of the press in Scotland and Wales don't seem to agree, but of course they themselves are ultimately subject to the control of the English political Establishment which thus restricts the right of free speech in Wales and Scotland.

While I accept the facts of the so-called "class war" and the need for the working class in various places and at various times to close ranks and pursue class warfare, in order to combat exploitation and to achieve a fairer distribution of wealth, I believe that in a participating democracy, social justice can be achieved with a minimum of the old class warfare, through legislation which ensures more participation and a much fairer distribution of wealth, and which outlaws what we in the SNP call "undue concentration of wealth" in a few hands. In fact, by treating everybody as workers and by putting the interests of the people as a whole before the interest of any one section, and especially by spending far more of the nation's wealth on educating our people in social responsibilities and in the value and pleasures of cultural pursuits, we can gradually eradicate these class barriers. In other words, I am not active in the SNP just to get an independent Parliament in Scotland, I am in the SNP to try and play a part in securing a better Scotland for succeeding generations, free in every way which is morally justifiable. Consequently, I feel an obligation to be able to say to the electorate how the SNP wants to see Scotland run, and I have no doubt that the majority of the members of the Party agree with me. It was such a belief which inspired hundreds of people in 1968 and 1969 to give up so much time and to make so much effort, so that we could place before the electorate at the 1970 General Election a manifesto which reflected our understanding of, as well as our concern for, the needs and the wishes of the people of Scotland.

Perhaps we tackled an impossible task, as one can see by looking at the agenda for a meeting of the National Assembly held on 18th and 19th January 1969. The Agenda included many items dealing with routine or organisational matters, such as the convenership of committees, but its main concern included the following:

133

Restatements of policy on Natural Resources, Transport and Broadcasting.

A report that National Council had accepted the policies drafted by the Assembly on Agriculture and Horticulture, on Forestry and on Industrial Development.

Detailed reports and drafts from the Policy Committees dealing with the Scottish Constitution, Forestry, Fuel and Power, Natural Resources, Industrial Development, Welfare and Community Services, Manpower and Employment, Transport, and Education.

Progress reports from the Committees dealing with Local Government, Finance and Taxation, Fisheries, Housing, Health Services, External Affairs, Defence, Science and Technology, the Arts, Broadcasting, Sport and Recreation, and Tourism.

What force impelled so many of us to work so hard on such things? Nothing short of belief in a future of contentment and prosperity and dignity for a Scotland with self-government. The success at Hamilton and in the local authority elections spurred us on in the belief and the hope that the Scottish people would respond by electing SNP Members of Parliament at the 1970 General Election.

Had we been able to convey to the electorate our enthusiasm, our honesty of purpose and our grasp of Scottish affairs, we would undoubtedly have had several M.P.s returned. Why did we win in the Western Isles, where our candidate was Donald Stewart, serving the community in his third term as Provost of Stornoway? A lot of the factors involved are unrecorded and cannot be estimated but there is one factor which I am sure told in Donald Stewart's favour. He and his fellow members of the Party had worked away steadily for years in their communities and they were well known and established citizens who represented the SNP as a living body of respected people. They were not just faces or words on leaflets or in newspaper columns but real people whom the electorate felt they could trust. Other factors which I am sure are important, are that the vast majority of the electors in the Western Isles are, in their communities, more Scottish than the often quasi-anglicised communities of central Scotland, and that the voters in the Outer Hebrides were not exposed to the same volume of anti-SNP propaganda which the Establishment Parties projected from the television screen whenever they had an opportunity.

However, in 1969, we were given an opportunity to canvass an electorate for support—in the Gorbals by-election—an electorate of only 33,000. We put all the effort we could into that election, and that amounted to almost total saturation in repeated canvassing, bill-posting, loud-speaking, leafleting and so on. The literature was first-class, we had songs with their roots in Gorbals and we had as candidate a young Glasgow Town Councillor, pugnacious and forthright, with a reputation for getting things done.

Although a scientific and neutral survey of the electorate, started long before the campaign was under way, showed that nearly 70% of the people were in favour of self-government, our share of the poll was 25%. In fact, this was slightly more than the survey predicted we would get. Why did people not vote for the SNP?—"because you are not strong enough yet." That was the simple straightforward answer of the majority of the sympathisers who did not vote for us.

In that constituency, there were hundreds of people living in conditions worse than animals. We claimed some of their votes, but perhaps those with generations of hopelessness behind them regarded us as too new, too inexperienced, and possibly too bright and shiny to have any real concern for them. The vast majority of those who did live in decent houses gave the credit for their improved circumstances entirely to the Labour Party, perhaps not unjustly, but they did not see that the Labour Party of Harold Wilson and Frank McElhone is not the Labour Party of Tom Johnston and Alice Cullen, the Labour M.P. whose death had made the by-election necessary.

The situation was not comparable with the situation in Hamilton two years earlier. We had been in the glare of publicity for two years and our opponents had recognised us as a threat to their power base. We are the only national Scottish party but, in Gorbals in 1969 and throughout Scotland in 1970, the choice between voting for Scotland and voting for England was not successfully conveyed to the electorate. As a Party, we have always avoided the obvious pitfalls of appearing anti-English. To say that one does not want Scotland run by an English Parliament can be so easily construed as an unfriendly attitude to the English people that most of us have talked about "Westminster" or "Whitehall" or "London." I think that the time has come for the people of Scotland to realise that the choice is not, as we have often said, "for or against Scotland." It is "for Scotland or for England."

The disappointment at not winning Gorbals did little, if anything, to reduce the Party's effort. Gorbals had been Labour for 51 years and to many members a win would have indeed been a miracle. Before polling in Gorbals, we knew we had another by-election on our hands—South Ayrshire, following the death of the redoubtable Emrys Hughes, a Welshman who had married Keir Hardie's daughter and who had represented the constituency for a generation, in a distinguished and often rebellious radical career. Winifred Ewing was very saddened by the loss of the only M.P. from Scotland who had consistently shown her support and friendship in the House of Commons.

Compared with Gorbals, South Ayrshire posed a lot of problems for us. In Glasgow we had been able to muster sufficient Party workers to run a first-class campaign and to provide an excellent electoral machine on polling day; but South Ayrshire was just a bit too far away for the vast majority of SNP activists. We knew that our strength in Ayrshire was low, especially in the constituency itself. I had long accepted the theory that the SNP did well in an atmosphere of hope and that in depressed areas with high unemployment, bad housing and other poor social conditions, we did not do as well. This theory has been borne out in comparable situations in other countries, and it certainly seems to have been proved in Scotland. The depressed mining villages of South Ayrshire, with a bleak and hopeless outlook, made a better battle-ground for the traditional class war than for the radical reforms of a Party seeking what seemed to be such a distant thing as a parliament for Scotland.

Our candidate had been Emrys Hughes' Election Agent in 1966, Sam Purdie, a Colliery Engineer who, after winning a scholarship to Ruskin College, Oxford, was in his final year at Strathclyde University, studying Economics.

The Labour Party's tactics in fighting against the challenge of the SNP in South Ayrshire were of the kind familiar to SNP workers in West Lothian and later to become so to those in Hamilton—they amounted to little more than a campaign of smearing the SNP candidate. Possibly the attacks were the more vicious because Sam Purdie had, without losing integrity or conviction, left the Labour Party and joined the Scottish National Party. Sam Purdie never stooped to the mud-slinging level of the Labour opposition. He had no airs or graces and showed himself to be competent above average in his knowledge of people, politics and economics.

At our first attempt in this constituency, we won 20% of

the poll; the draw from the Labour poll was 13% and from the Tory poll 7%. The *Scots Independent* commented after the result: "The campaign in South Ayrshire was almost entirely a South Ayrshire effort. Certainly, our H.Q. staff helped considerably with guidance and help in organisation and publicity, but the Election Agent, Charles Lawson, and all the others who unselfishly threw themselves into the campaign for weeks and months, carried the full weight of the canvassing with little sustained effort from outside. This result was, like the Gorbals result, a disappointment for those who thought that the Hamilton result would inevitably lead to the winning of more seats."

In the course of the South Ayrshire campaign, two questions of importance were dealt with by the Party. One of them received a surprising amount of coverage—the statement re-affirming our belief that an independent Scotland would associate with the other states of the British Isles in co-operation in economic, social, cultural and scientific fields. This had been Party policy for years and had been resuscitated at National Council in 1969 in reaction to being harrassed by cries of "isolationists" and "separatists" by the English parties. It certainly did not alter in any way the aims or fundamental policies of the Party.

At the time I said, "We do not seek as part of our independence a package deal that would cut us off from our neighbours. There is no reason why an independent Scotland managing her own affairs and in control of her own finances should not have a customs and passport union with the other states of the British Isles and have other forms of co-operation also. It would be illogical not to do so. Independence for Scotland will produce an outward looking, international Scotland."

The other matter concerned international affairs on a wider scale. Throughout Scotland we had mounted a strong campaign against British entry into the Common Market. Mrs Ewing had asked many questions in Parliament and we had learned that no one representing Scotland in the Labour Government and no one from Scotland in the Tory or Liberal Parties and no one from St Andrew's House had raised a finger in Scotland's interests in the Common Market negotiations which were being so avidly pursued on behalf of the Labour Government by an M.P. from Scotland, Mr George Thomson.

We decided to send a delegation to Brussels to hold discussions with the Common Market Commission in which we would put our view of the U.K. Government's decision to re-open

137

negotiations for entry to the Common Market. We wanted to make it clear that Scotland was a nation and that for England to take Scotland into the Common Market without consulting the people of Scotland would be a further breach of the Act of Union. George Leslie, as Senior Vice-Chairman, went as leader of the delegation which consisted of Winifred Ewing, James Halliday and Douglas Crawford. This was a very strong team. James Halliday was convener of the External Affairs Committee of the Party at the time. A Lecturer in the teaching of History at Dundee College of Education, he had been Chairman of the Party before Arthur Donaldson. He is one of the Party's finest orators and writers.

The delegation held press conferences and was widely reported in European newspapers and on radio and television. Winifred Ewing appeared on television in the Netherlands and Douglas Crawford in Belgium. The session with the senior officials of the Common Market revealed their ignorance of Scotland. They had no idea of the depth of feeling in Scotland against Britain going into the Market, and knew nothing about the SNP.

The most important thing the delegation achieved was to successfully draw attention to the fact that the Scottish National Party was again serving notice on the other countries of Europe that there was a strong and growing movement in Scotland for independence, and that a Scottish Parliament would not feel itself bound by any treaties and agreements entered into on behalf of the people of Scotland by any British Government.

Most of the people who opposed entry into the Common Market did it on almost instinctive grounds. Professional economists and politicians disagreed among themselves, irrespective of political convictions, as to whether entry would be good or bad. The discussions within the Scottish National Party following the return of our delegation to Brussels clarified our view of the Common Market and consequently hardened our opposition to it. Ours was essentially a political view.

In April 1970, when addressing a meeting in Paisley, I said: "We have been skilfully persuaded to think of the Common Market in economic trading terms only as a way of bringing the nations of Europe into the still waters of peace and prosperity. However, over the years, the Scottish National Party and other vigilant people, in England as well as in Scotland, have called attention to dangers which we believe could chill these waters. In fact, we now see clearly that the double-talk of the Common Market is covering up more than a few stray ice-floes. The distinct shape of political centralism which is now clearly over the horizon is an iceberg and we have seen only the tip of its dangerous and destructive might. It threatens to crash into Western Europe and destroy all the ideals of national freedom and national identity which Western Europe has developed, often painfully, over the past 700 years. These ideals, the principles of participating democracy and modern nation-hood, were born here in Scotland. We must defend them.

"The SNP delegation which went to Brussels has confirmed our view that it is the aim of the Common Market to establish political domination of the whole of Western Europe and to tolerate no deviations from this line. The Common Marketeers of today are as much doctrinaire centralists as their opposite numbers in the Kremlin in Moscow. Their political philosophy is insidious to those who are steeped in the democratic tradition. They say 'To be big is to be good; to be bigger is to be better; to be biggest is to be supreme. To be centralised is to be efficient; to be a Common Market organisation man is to be one of Euprope's chosen people.' It is no accident that the English Parties have indicated their strong wish to go into the Common Market. To do so is a logical continuation of their centralist thinking which has been so damaging to Scotland's people and to Scotland's economy."

A day or two before making that speech, I was in Arbroath at a Party Rally to celebrate the 650th anniversary of the signing of the famous Declaration of Independence. The actual date of the anniversary was Monday, 6th April, when the Establishment had a service in the ruins of the abbey. We had our ceremony on the nearest Saturday, 4th April, but we were not allowed to assemble in the precincts of the abbey. What looked like about half of the County of Angus Police Force turned out to make sure that we stayed beyond the railings. The nearest we got in the course of our ceremonies was when Jim McGugan, who had taken the part of King Robert the Bruce in the Arbroath Pageant and was prospective SNP candidate for North Angus and Mearns, went along with his brother, Stuart, to lay our newly-signed Declaration of Nationhood at the great West Door of the ruins of the abbey.

The wording of our Declaration was largely the work of Michael Grieve: ". . . the time has now come for the people of Scotland to assert their rights and to accept once again their full responsibility as a nation.

139

"In recent years the fabric of Scotland has been openly under deliberate attack. There has been no physical coercion but centralisation has accelerated erosion of responsibility on all the distinctive fronts of national life and endeavour, as a process of assimilation has been vigorously pursued.

"Yet Scotland still possesses today almost all the attributes of a sovereign nation except a parliament.

"To the other nations of the world we say this: We look forward to the time in the near future when the people of Scotland, with independence restored, will apply to take their place among you, willing and ready to accept their full responsibility to humanity."

When elected Chairman in Oban in 1969, I had promised the Party that I would visit the maximum number of constituencies possible before the General Election. Eleven months later, I had been to 30 or more out of the 71. I found it a colossal task. As the General Election neared, I became so single-minded about the campaign that, looking back, I'm sure that my wife and children and my colleagues at work had difficulty in getting through to me regarding other responsibilities.

A pitfall of which I had become aware was undue concentration by members and branches on economic and social policies to the exclusion of propaganda for self-government. As we faced the burgh elections and the county council elections at the beginning of May, I realised from reports coming in that the Labour Party were making an unprecedented effort in canvassing and in election preparations. To them, of course, it was an integral part of their campaign for the General Election which they knew would almost certainly be within a few weeks of the local elections. In the early stages of the campaign, I issued a warning not to fall into the traps set by our opponents who wanted us to play down our appeal to national self-respect, in order to weaken our effectiveness.

By playing the Labour and Tory Party game of appealing emotionally to immediate self-interest or sectional interest or greed or fear, we became in many places almost indistinguishable from the English Parties—just another party with promises and plugs. Nevertheless, even in places like the burgh of Whitburn, where we had always followed a strong line on Scottish Independence, the Party suffered losses, even while scoring, as we did in Whitburn, 47% of the poll.

I made some rather caustic comments on the results: "Just as one weak link spoils a chain, the lack of self-discipline or the seeking of publicity rather than the good of the community on the part of one councillor can spoil the good work done by fifty other councillors. In many councils throughout the country, the SNP has worked well and earned respect and support thereby, but their work has been undermined by bad publicity for others. I am confident that the Party has learned its lesson." The lesson, of course, was much too close to the General Election for our comfort.

We had parliamentary candidates in all but six of the constituencies—Orkney and Shetland, where our Constituency Association deemed it inexpedient to contest against Mr Grimond, and five constituencies where our organisation was so short of manpower or cash or both that they felt unable to contest: Edinburgh North, Rutherglen, Cathcart, Kelvingrove and Greenock. We had a panel of candidates at least as capable as those of any other party. Their average age was thirty-eight as against forty-two for the Conservatives and forty-six in the Labour Party. With ten women standing for the SNP, we were a long way from equal participation of the sexes, but we had the highest number of women candidates of any party.

Douglas Crawford made valiant efforts to get news coverage and, in accordance with the pattern which I remarked on earlier, the *Aberdeen Press and Journal* and *The Scotsman* gave fair coverage to our statements, speeches and news items. The same could be said of Grampian Television which was the only network to feature the SNP on a par with the other parties in the last week of the Election Campaign, when it showed an hour-long discussion programme in which a representative from each of the parties contesting within the Grampian region took part.

The other newspapers assisted the promotion of their chosen parties—*The Glasgow Herald, The Dundee Courier* and the *Scottish Daily Express* tending to support the Tory Party while the *Daily Record* faithfully blew the trumpets for Harold Wilson & Co. Of greater importance than the newspaper coverage was the television coverage. We had representatives taking part in discussion programmes and I made a five-minute party political broadcast on television in the course of the campaign, but we were totally excluded from what we rated as the most important part of television coverage—the daily coverage in the main news programmes from the electoral headquarters of the other parties and the daily "focus" programmes on current political topics.

It was significant too that B.B.C. and S.T.V., whether by chance or design, did not have a programme in which the SNP could have taken part in the last week of the Election. The fact is that without television coverage we did not rate with the other parties in the eyes of the vast majority of TV-oriented voters; not because we hadn't something valuable to say or to add to discussion; nor because they did not want self-government for Scotland; but as the voters of Gorbals replied in the survey which we made in 1969, "You are not strong enough yet."

An experience of my own West Lothian campaign reinforces the foregoing conclusions. In one of the areas of West Lothian where we had not done very well previously but where we believed there was a potential for improvement, we did a special canvass ten days before polling day.

On this particular occasion, we mustered a team of experienced canvassers from all over the County and canvassed everyone who was at home that night, keeping careful records. Those who claimed to be definitely voting SNP totalled over 35% which, compared with our previous results in this area, was very good. A return visit to the area after the General Election indicated that we had been given support of 24%. An analysis of the reasons given for not voting SNP reflected what we had found in the Gorbals and elsewhere, that the people lacked confidence in the Party because they did not hear us and see us on television, on a par with the other parties.

Our experience in this one area was echoed not only in West Lothian but in many other constituencies. Our disappointment at the result in West Lothian was tempered by our realisation that the percentage drop of the share in the poll in West Lothian was almost exactly the same as in Hamilton and in the other constituencies in Central Scotland which the Party had contested in 1966.

The bitterest blow, of course, was Hamilton. Winifred Ewing had been an exceptionally active and conscientious M.P. She had been more effective than any other single person had ever been in attacking the Establishment Parties where they liked it least—in the heart of their very select club—the English House of Commons. I heard the Hamilton result in the S.T.V. studios in Glasgow where I was representing the Party in the programme covering the results. Angus McGillveray had accompanied me to Glasgow, having taken me round the polling stations in West Lothian during the day. The West Lothian count had still to take place on the Friday morning. Our time in the S.T.V. studios had not given us much comfort, what with the loss of Hamilton and the poor city results for the SNP.

At about 4 a.m. on the Friday, Angus and I drove to a house in Hamilton where a quiet little company was trying to absorb the unpalatable fact that the electorate of Hamilton had rejected Winifred Ewing and the Scottish National Party. It was a poignant scene. Mrs Ewing had yet to shed any tears. She had fought so hard, surpassing the standards of commitment and effort of practically every other M.P. from Scotland. It was disappointing but it was not defeat. She had held her vote. The result had turned on Labour increasing its vote to a record poll. The loss of a battle is not the loss of a war, and we knew that we were still in the early stages of the effort.

At the West Lothian count on the Friday morning the result was clear after only a few ballot boxes had been emptied. We still had a good vote, over 15,000, but such reassurance for the future was not much comfort at the time. A car was ready to take me back to the S.T.V. programme for the remainder of the Friday afternoon. Apart from a catnap on the Thursday evening, I had been on the go since before 5 a.m. on the Thursday but I could not possibly have gone to sleep before knowing the result in one particular constituency, the Western Isles. Mrs Ewing had come into the studio in Glasgow for the end of the S.T.V. programme. When it ended we returned to her home and waited, quiet and apprehensive. Donald Stewart 'phoned early in the evening to say that he thought he "would maybe tip him over" —"him" being the portly figure of Malcolm MacMillan, M.P. for the constituency since 1935. I answered the telephone when it rang later in the evening. It was Donald. "I'm in," he said, shattering instantly the subdued atmosphere in the room, transforming it into bright hope and noisy jubilation.

The voters of the Western Isles had given the lead to the rest of Scotland. Theirs was the last result to come in, bringing the Scottish National Party its first ever victory in a General Election. The next day, at Bannockburn, we held our annual commemoration of the victorious battle at which the right of the people of Scotland to run their own affairs independent of English tyranny was established. Donald Stewart's win suffused the occasion with a wonderful warmth, marred only by one very sad recollection. This was the first Bannockburn parade for 40 years without Matt Ferguson of Renfrew as the Party's Standard-bearer. His erect and dignified figure had been present in that capacity on 93 occasions. He died in April 1970. His successor was Ron Fraser of Edinburgh, a man who was big of heart and big of frame. Nothing for Scotland was too much trouble for

143

him, and the tragedy of his death after a road accident in 1972 robbed the Party of a worthy successor to Matt Ferguson and cast a cloud of sorrow over his many friends.

At the foot of Pilkington Jackson's magnificent statue of Robert the Bruce, the feeling was of a family gathering. There were nearly four thousand people present, practically every one of whom had been active, some at an almost killing pace, for weeks in the campaign. In the chair was Arthur Donaldson who had fought a wonderful campaign in Galloway, the SNP's first in the constituency, claiming over 20% of the poll. Winifred Ewing, Robert McIntyre and I all addressed the crowd. There was a tremendously purposeful atmosphere at that gathering. We were very happy at the result in the Western Isles and in having another ten seats in which we had over 20% of the poll. The marks of the fight for freedom were in our hearts as well as in our tired bodies and sleep-starved minds. We had done our best. We could do no more.

In sending the thanks of the Party to Donald Stewart, to the team that worked for his success, and to the voters who had the good sense to elect him, I told him of the Bannockburn Rally at which we had been proud to have one of his constituents, Miss Margaret Morrison, to represent him at the head of the parade.

"In being elected," I wrote, "you have lifted our hopes which, although not dashed by the loss of Hamilton and by setbacks in other constituencies, were not nearly as high as they are now with the prospect of you speaking for us at Westminster."

CHAPTER 10

TAKING STOCK AND TAKING ACTION, 1970-71

T HE NEXT THREE MONTHS were extremely busy for me. The election did not release me from political obligations; in fact, the reverse seemed to be the case. We had fought throughout Scotland for the first time, and there was a mass of material to examine and analyse.

A week after the election I wrote to the other 64 candidates asking for their impressions of the contest. What I wanted was their opinion on the three greatest difficulties encountered in the campaign, and the three most important factors to be considered in our plans for the future. The response was good, and helped me considerably in drafting plans for submission to the Party.

On the political front, Douglas Crawford and I looked for subjects on which we could take the initiative. We had credibility as far as the Common Market was concerned. We also highlighted the ironic position of the political representation from Scotland. The people of Scotland voted for a Labour government, returning forty-four Labour M.P.s with twenty-three Tories, three Liberals, and Nationalist Donald Stewart making up the balance of the seventy-one Scottish seats. In fact, had representation been proportional to votes cast for parties, no party would have had an overall majority. The figures would have been Labour 32, Conservative 27, Scottish National Party eight and Liberal four. This is a more accurate reflection of how the people of Scotland voted in 1970 and is a strong argument for the introduction of the single transferable vote system, as proposed by the SNP.

The fact that the Scots had voted for Harold Wilson's team, in spite of their abysmal record in six years of mis-government, was about the most unpalatable aspect of the General Election results. Nevertheless, the people had chosen a Labour Government, and had instead to thole a Tory Government. However, the authoritarian leadership of the Labour Party in Scotland must have been pleased, especially the Chairman of the Party's Scottish Council, Mr John Pollock, who had publicly stated to the Crowther Commission, before the General Election, that the Labour Party in Scotland preferred Tory rule from London to a Scottish Labour Government in Edinburgh. Such people apparently want to see Scottish nationhood eradicated. John Pollock is a Scottish schoolmaster. Is it likely the children in his care will learn to appreciate the value of their Scottish nationality? One might accept a playing down of nationalism in relation to Scottish matters if internationalism was preached; but the fact is that our children are taught English history and traditions in place of Scottish.

This denial of their Scottish origins and spirit by the leaders of the Labour Party in Scotland is only one sign of the great betrayal of the principles on which the radical and Labour movements were founded. Not only is the Labour Party extremely vulnerable on its record on Scotland—*e.g.* the loss of 65,000 jobs for men in the course of their six years in office— they are also wide open to criticism on the application of their so-called internationalist outlook, *e.g.* the Kenya Asians Bill, the Commonwealth Immigrants Act, the sell-out on Rhodesia, their support of nuclear bases, U.S. and British, in Scotland, their diabolical two-faced participation in the Biafran War in which war materials went to both sides from Britain, and the continued supply of military equipment to South Africa. What on earth would the distinguished Clydeside M.P.s of the 1920s and 1930s have thought of their brethren in power in the 1960s? Would John MacLean have approved of their efforts for the working people of Scotland? Never.

The work of the SNP between the General Election of 1970 and our Annual Conference in October of that year was, apart from routine activity, mainly concerned with an assessment of the General Election results and discussion of how we could most effectively proceed in the years ahead. The National Executive Committee considered lengthy memoranda from me which I had distilled from collective experience all over Scotland. A special report called "The Next Four Years" was drawn up and circulated twice for discussion throughout the whole Party—once for National Council and then again for Annual Conference. My main concern was to ensure that bone-picking and head-scratching after the Election were not prolonged unnecessarily and that clear guidelines were agreed by the whole Party in preparation for the succeeding General Election.

At our Conference in October 1970, we were far from being downhearted. Most of the journalists and other observers noted this and some were surprised. To them and to the world at large, I made it quite clear where we were going, and how.

"The challenge to us and the whole nation of Scots is a great adventure—the adventure not only of being a nation again, but of being a new nation. We have a heritage on which to build as a people. We have a heritage of which other people could be envious. We in the Scottish National Party, as the spearhead of this movement, must make ourselves more knowledgeable about our heritage and we must educate our members and supporters in these things which are fundamental to the cultural, spiritual and social well-being of the people of Scotland.

"In our heritage we find a key to our outlook summed up in the words 'radical' and 'egalitarian.' That key to our past is the key to our future. We are essentially a democratic people. Scotland has spread much radical thought in the world down the centuries. Such thought was reflected in a formal document 650 years ago in the Declaration of Arbroath. These sentiments were later expressed in the philosophical writings of George Buchanan and others and in poetry and song. Scotland's talent for unorthodox and radical thinking also revealed itself in the Reformation and in the desire to provide universal education.

"Scotland played a leading rôle in the European Enlightenment. Adam Smith instituted the modern discipline of economics. David Hume brought empirical methods to bear on the study of man and society. Scots have been inventors and innovators in science, engineering, medicine, architecture, mining and manufacturing. Men like Keir Hardie, John MacLean and James Maxton were in the forefront of the radical Labour movement when it was a genuine movement for social justice and not the pitiful caricature we know today.

"Given the chance, Scots and Scotland could continue to give to the world, but if the sources of inspiration disappear, if the nation is emasculated and cut off from its traditions, Scotland will have nothing to give the world except scenery and servility. When we can hold our heads up and say "I am a Scot" with all the dignity of full nationhood, we as a nation will be in a position to interact with other nations to our mutual benefit.

"These things all constitute part of the great urge of this Party. It is not surprising that the SNP represents a growing number of Scots who long for a cosmopolitan Scotland and who totally reject the provincial rôle and status into which Westminster and its camp-followers are trying to cast us.

"We are not just concerned with a solitary aim, although

147

that aim of independence is over-riding and is fundamentally the greatest thing we can fight for—freedom. We are part of a social movement as well, agitating for reforms. The strands of those who seek cultural regeneration in Scotland are also working within the Scottish National Party. We are all working together woven into a strong fabric like a tartan. We reflect colours— different outlooks, different disciplines and differences of character and temperament. But a tartan is a perfectly balanced pattern—it has a disciplined design and, of course, it has an identity and the identity we have is that of the nation of Scotland.

"Had the whole nation been thus bound together with such a common aim, what would we not have achieved in the twentieth century had we had self-government sixty years ago? Instead of stagnating and drifting backwards, held down by the burden of London's continuing imperial paternalism and pretensions, and bled of people and possessions, we Scots might have achieved the strong economic growth of Finland and Norway, the cultural vigour of Denmark, and the conquest of poverty and deprivation that we see in Sweden.

"Instead of being tarnished with a shared image of the "sick man of Europe," instead of having to share English foreign policies, Scotland could have worked first of all to build a more prosperous country, to look after its children, its sick and old people, and ensure a fairer distribution of wealth; and beyond that we would have been working for world co-operation and peace side by side with the Scandinavian democracies and the other small nations of the world.

"We will never get the reforms we want from London, or from Brussels. We will get these things only when the Scottish people support the SNP. We are committed totally to the democratic method, civilised and non-violent. But as it becomes increasingly obvious to us that there are well-entrenched vested interests who hate the thought of independence for Scotland, and who influence the Labour and Tory Parties accordingly, we will be moved to protest more volubly and more significantly to draw the attention of the people to social and economic injustices such as emigration, unemployment and inadequate housing, and to the manipulation of power and privilege which has barred the SNP from a fair share of television time and prevented us from putting our case to the people of Scotland. We must protest vigorously so that the people of Scotland will realise that we are prepared to act as well as to talk.

"The outlook of this Party is a distillation of outlooks,

148

essentially radical and egalitarian, in accordance with Scottish humanitarian traditions which have little to do with British party political labels. The mainspring of our dedication is love of humanity in general and of Scotland in particular. Any love which is pure, any love which lifts the heart and soul must inevitably contain an element of sacrifice.

"Something has to be given up in order to achieve what is seen to be a greater and worthier goal. The lesser has to be absorbed in the greater. That is why being conservative, liberal or socialist is of secondary importance within the Scottish National Party. Once we have our own parliament with Scottish general elections, people will have a choice of voting for whatever Scottish political parties are in existence at that time, but until then, we must put Scotland first and vote for independence.

"There is no question of the over-riding aim of self-government and independence being diminished in any way because we make proposals as to what a Scottish Government should do about this or that. On the contrary, adding knowledge of industrial development, housing, education, fishing or any other subject to our claim for independence enhances our chances of gaining the confidence of the people.

"What we have got to do in the next three or four years is to weld our policies together in a radical, philosophical outlook on how Scotland should look after her own affairs.

"We are engaged in the greatest cause in the world—the cause of freedom. We have a beautiful country. We have honourable traditions. We are radical and cosmopolitan in our outlook. We seek with humility to play such part as we can in international affairs but, first of all, we want to put matters right here, at home, in Scotland."

1970 brought the 150th Anniversary of an event of which the vast majority of people in Scotland know nothing. I myself was numbered among the ignorant. I knew more about the philosophical and political struggles of the late eighteenth and early nineteenth centuries in France and England and Ireland than of contemporaneous and similar occurrences in Scotland. I had heard of Thomas Muir of Huntershill and his banishment as a convict because he had voiced the grievances of the poor and the exploited of Scotland and had urged political reform. Because the movement for "liberty, equality and fraternity" emanated from France, with whom Britain was at war, the cries of Muir and many others were labelled traitorous and seditious and consequently they were dealt with very harshly.

The gap in the knowledge of this period in Scottish history was partly filled in 1970 with a very welcome volume on the Radical Rising of 1820. Fortunately there are students who are now engaged in looking even further into this crucial period in the political history of Scotland. The three martyrs of 1820—Wilson, Hardie and Baird—were devout Christians, typically representative of the Scottish working classes of the period. They were not ashamed to die for freedom. Looking back, one can clearly identify the source of the oppression against which they fought as English imperialism, aided and abetted by the Scottish land-owning and capitalist classes which, in the main, were subservient to English domination.

In September 1970, I went for the first time to a Commemoration Service in Sighthill Cemetery in Glasgow along with twenty or thirty others to recall the sacrifice of these martyrs and their cry "Scotland free, or a desert."

In 1971 and again in 1972, on a Sunday in September, I returned to Sighthill Cemetery. The committee which runs the services consists really of one man—John Murphy of Paisley—whose transparent goodness and dedication make him the friend of all sections of the national movement in Scotland. The 1820 commemorations are not SNP affairs although the majority of those present on each occasion have been members of the Scottish National Party. It is a meeting-ground on which all who believe in freedom and in the right of the people of Scotland to self-government can meet without acrimony. At the 1970 meeting, I heard Winifred Ewing make one of her best speeches —and she made it at two minutes' notice.

A man who has spoken each year is Michael Donnelly, who has done much research into a hitherto badly charted section of Scotland's history. At the 1972 service, he told us of a general strike in Glasgow of some 60,000 to 65,000 workers in support of the 1820 Rising. "It lasted from 3rd to 7th April 1820 and was only abandoned when all hope of supporting action south of the Border was ruled out. This strike was not only the first general strike in industrial history, but the first political general strike. It was called for a political purpose on the orders of the Provisional Government of the Radicals, rather than for the usual economic reasons." It is not Scotland's only first in such matters. In 1870, miners in Fife won the first eight-hour day anywhere in the world as the result of a strike. The annals of the trade union and labour movements in Scotland must surely provide a great deal of material for work on the history of radicalism in Scotland. Yet such martyrdom and such initiative are barely recognised by the present Trade Union hierarchy in Scotland, who recall events and people outside of Scotland and often ignore those who were Scots.

One of the difficulties which the Scottish National Party has experienced is the bond between the trade union movement and the Labour Party. It is quite understandable how that bond developed. It is also quite understandable that it is sometimes stretched to the limit by the wavering opportunism of the Labour Party, but it is traditional and such traditions die hard.

Scotland is fortunate that it has its own Trade Union Congress, but the total rejection by the Labour Party of any approach other than what they call British, which is really an English approach, strictly limits the effectiveness of the S.T.U.C. in political terms. It has no place in the Labour Party Constitution.

Scotland has more trade unionists in proportion to its population than England and most other countries, but it took the 1970 General Election result to make me comprehend fully the political importance of this section of the population.

The Party started the Association of Scottish Nationalist Trade Unionists in the early 60s under the leadership of William Johnston who was Parliamentary candidate for the SNP in East Dumbarton in 1966. He is in the tradition of John MacLean— a socialist with his faith pinned on Scotland. His attitude was summed up in an article he wrote for the *Scots Independent* rejecting the "one nation" philosophy expounded by the English T.U.C. General Secretary, Victor Feather, during the U.C.S. crisis. "For too long the Scottish Trade Union movement has swallowed the opium of this one nation philosophy. Wilhelm Leibknecht said, 'All unity is not strength. The unity of a lamb and a lion ends in the lamb being devoured by the lion.' This applies to Scotland and England. The prosperity of our English Trade Union brothers derives from centralisation of industry at the expense of Scottish closures.

"The wages of English workers vary from 5% to 25% higher than those of their Scottish counterparts. The unemployment rate in England is, on average, half the figure for Scotland. Immigration is the English problem. Emigration is the ruin of Scotland. One nation? No, Mr Feather, one nation perpetrating economic imperialism on another—that same philosophy and economic programme that England's other colonies tore asunder."

For years, William Johnston was almost a lone Trade Unionist voice in the S.N.P. I can remember him urging me in 1966 to look to the Trade Unions for more support for the Scottish National Party. I accepted what he said but we did nothing practical about it. Then, in June 1970, realising that in spite of the by-election victory at Hamilton, in spite of Winifred Ewing's non-stop and valiant efforts, in spite of very active involvement in local authority work in West Lothian, in spite of a sustained and expensive and well-run SNP election campaign, the Labour vote in West Lothian had held firm, yielding us no more than we had previously won.

What was wrong? The answer was quite simple—the average Trade Unionist, although very sympathetic to the idea, did not have sufficient confidence in a self-governing Scotland or, if he did have confidence in it, he was still to be convinced that the Scottish National Party was capable of achieving independence and providing an effective and reliable provisional government thereafter.

So I had meetings with William Johnston and with others, and by early 1971 a re-formed Association was under way with members from all over Scotland who were prepared to take a lead with the main aim of furthering within the Trade Union movement the belief that only by having a parliament in Scotland will there be any chance of realising their basic aims. The Association provided a flow of ideas in two directions, from the Trade Union movement into the Party and from the Party into the Trade Union movement. The Association was to encourage members of the Party to take a full and constructive part in all the normal activities of the Trade Union movement.

1971 certainly saw some significant happenings on the industrial front in Scotland. The first received very little publicity. It was a strike in March in the Scott-McQuay factory in Hillington, owned by the Sterne Group. It was not a routine wage-claim strike. The men were demanding the right to work in Scotland. They had been offered a move to England, or other jobs in the area, as the work they were doing, which was known to be very profitable, was to be transferred to a factory in England. The men struck in protest against the closure, and in favour of the Scottish branch factory being kept in operation.

Along with William Johnston, I visited the men on strike and we took what action we could to aid them with publicity

152

and other support. Unfortunately there was not time for the strike to be made official by the unions involved and it was not successful in its aim of retaining the jobs in Scotland, but it was the forerunner of a much greater effort, also based on demanding the right to work in Scotland, the U.C.S. work-in.

The SNP backed the men of U.C.S. from the word "go." I went to Clydebank to meet the Shop Stewards and pledge the Party's support. This was by no means the first time that the SNP had been involved in the shipbuilding industry in Clydeside.

During the 60s, we produced tens of thousands of leaflets urging support for massive Government investment in modernisation of Clyde shipbuilding. We had been involved in meetings with Trade Union leaders and Shop Stewards on earlier occasions, but of course none matched the importance of the U.C.S. work-in. Several of the Shop Stewards in the yards were SNP members, the best-known being a Clydebank Councillor, Ian Smith. Many SNP branches ran special functions to raise money for the Shop Stewards' Fund. In relation to the great needs of the work-in, the SNP contribution must have been very small, but it did identify the Party throughout Scotland with the stand of the Clydesiders.

The climax of the U.C.S. campaign was the great rally on Glasgow Green. The support of the SNP was recognised and I was invited by the Shop Stewards to speak on behalf of the Scottish National Party. In the walk from George Square, I was accompanied by William Johnston, my philosophical friend and mentor and, on this occasion, his presence was almost required as a bodyguard. This recognition of the SNP was strongly resented by some of the more bigoted and blind loyalists of the Labour Party; but the U.C.S. leaders were not concerned with narrow-minded party dogma. The rally had the spirit of a movement and the Shop Stewards welcomed the participation of all who whole-heartedly pledged support.

Most of my speech was well received—"We can no longer remain a branch factory nation. We are no longer prepared to face closures and redundancies without any control over the ups and downs of the London-dominated economic mess. It is inconceivable that any Scottish Government would have allowed this country to rot in the way that it has. It is inconceivable that a country which, two generations ago, built more than half of the world's shipping, should be allowed to decline in the way that it has. It is inconceivable that any Scottish Government would brutally axe shipbuilding in the upper Clyde as this English Government proposes."

I referred to a half century of pious promises of jobs in the pipeline, "but now we have a body of men prepared to act, to fight for their jobs. Indeed they are fighting for all Scotland and all Scotland must back them, to force the Government to think again and to take effective steps to stop the erosion of creative employment in Scotland, erosion which is not peculiar to the present or past Tory Governments—manpower and jobs were destroyed under Harold Wilson as well." Not surprisingly, this remark produced a reaction from some Labour Party supporters in the crowd. Was it unfair of me to attack the Wilson Government when their No. 1 man in Scotland for the whole six years, Mr William Ross, was on the platform beside me? As far as he and other Labour Party men were concerned, including Mr Wedgwood-Benn who, more than any other person, held ministerial responsibility for the U.C.S. mess, I was a flaw in their "British" unity; which, after all, was as it should be.

The man whom the thousands had come to hear spoke with persuasive passion and clarity, James Reid, an orator with great gifts of understanding and of expression, in whom most Scots find an appeal to which they gladly respond. Such a competent public spokesman was an enormous asset to the U.C.S. campaign. I fancy, however, that the unifying power, if indeed any one person could be said to wield such power in the co-ordinating committee, was in the able hands of the resolute, uncompromising and friendly convener, James Airlie.

It was a team effort, of course, and as I said at the 1972 Annual Conference of the Party: "The most important single aspect of the work-in was that it could not have happened that way in England. The English of all classes may shout and bawl defiance at each other but they invariably settle for a compromise solution; but to the people of Scotland compromise is never an acceptable solution. Our refusal to compromise is a national trait the world has recognised for centuries. Agreement on concensus, yes; but compromise, no.

"The men of U.C.S. stood firm—uncompromising. The people of Scotland stood firm with them—uncompromising. And of all political parties, the SNP had no reason to be ashamed of the support it gave because the SNP also stood firm—uncompromising—alongside the militant workers who demanded the right to work in Scotland—not just the right to work anywhere but the right to work here.

154

"It was Scottish tradition, Scottish principle, Scottish determination and Scottish community spirit which won the day. Of course, there was support from England and many other countries. But the stand was on Clydeside and that was where the battle was won."

The third significant occurrence on the industrial front in 1971 was the occupation of the Plessey factory at Alexandria, Dumbartonshire. This affair was a colossal scandal. Had the occupation of the factory not taken place at the same time as the U.C.S. work-in, it would have received much more publicity. The factory had been government-owned, being a naval torpedo works. With flowery talk and promises galore—such as one of 2000 new jobs in a year—the Labour Government sold this public asset to private industry a few weeks before the 1970 General Election. The plant was valued at anything from £8 to £12 million. The Plessey Company purchased the entire factory and contents, including stocks and the right to manufacture the Mark 24 Torpedo at their Ilford factory in England, for a fraction of the estimated value.

One can reasonably doubt if Plessey ever intended to work the factory. They got such a bargain from the Labour Government that they could afford weeks, even months or years, of unprofitable operating, gradually running the work force down with a view to removing the valuable machinery, stock and plant to English factories. The official take-over was in January 1971. In May, a reduction of 300 jobs was announced. In July, a complete closure was announced with a total loss of 700 jobs. The Shop Stewards had been most responsible and thorough. They had gone through every possible procedure from the time of the first talk of closure in 1969, facing many rebuffs, until they reached a blank wall with no possible future, so they took over, determined that the factory would not be dismantled and that no machinery, metals or parts would leave without their consent.

The occupation again demonstrated the resolute demands of the people of Scotland for the right to work in Scotland. The patience of the men at the Plessey gate was rewarded. Plessey were forced to agree to turn the premises into an industrial estate in conjunction with a factory developer and jobs were guaranteed. As in the U.C.S. case, the SNP gave full moral support and as much practical encouragement and help as possible.

In all three cases, in Scott-McQuay, in U.C.S. and in Plessey, the men were acting politically from an entirely Scottish base.

Their party politics did not matter but their resolution to fight for dignity and fair-dealing did matter. If the example of these men getting their priorities right was followed throughout Scotland by people in all walks of life and with all kinds of responsibilities, we would have a Scottish Parliament established after the next General Election.

CHAPTER 11

LOOKING AHEAD

WHILE THE U.C.S. crisis was at its peak, the political parties were preparing for a parliamentary by-election in the constituency of Stirling, Falkirk and Grangemouth Burghs, in which the SNP had scored 14·5% in 1970. Our candidate was the Provost of Stirling, Robert McIntyre, the man who won Motherwell for the SNP in 1945 and is one of the wisest and most skilful leaders the Party has had. If the response to the appeal for workers in the SNP had come some weeks earlier the result would have been closer, and a win for the SNP was not beyond the bounds of possibility. As it was, the SNP vote doubled, the Labour vote was cut by 23%, and the Tory vote was halved. The press coverage of the election was strange. It was almost as if no one wanted to report what was going on. The result may not have made an impact which echoed in the news corridors for weeks but it certainly proved an encouragement to the Party throughout Scotland.

Possibly we confused the electorate in the Stirling Burghs by-election by campaigning on too many issues—U.C.S., the Common Market, the destruction of the whole fabric of local government, the disintegration of the Scottish steel industry, the indecision about developing the valuable deep water port facilities at Hunterston, the shelving of Oceanspan (the imaginative plan of the Scottish Council for developing the under-used resources of central Scotland) and, of course, the exploitation of the Scottish oil resources in the North Sea. We had started campaigning seriously on the subject of oil early in 1971.

Throughout 1972, we increased the tempo of our oil campaign under the direction of Gordon Wilson, who had resumed national responsibility within the Party as an Executive Vice-Chairman. It was natural that he should be the Party's choice to fight the by-election in Dundee East, vacated at the end of 1972 by the Labour M.P., George Thomson, on his appointment as a Commissioner in the Common Market. The prospects in the by-election were not as promising as those in the Stirling

157

Burghs by-election a year earlier. The Dundee seat was marginal. In 1970, Labour had held it with 48% of the poll; the Tory had taken 43% and SNP 9%. Our record in Dundee had not been very good, as already noted.

However, we had a nucleus of men and women who had been active in promoting the oil campaign in the constituency before the by-election came on the horizon. One of them, Alan McKinney, was chosen as Election Agent and Gordon Wilson started his regular trips to Scotland's third and most neglected city. The Party responded to the challenge of Dundee and members rallied to the support of our campaign from all over Scotland. In the event, significant progress was achieved with second place, only 1141 votes behind Labour. The SNP share of the 1970 poll was more than tripled and the city's Conservative Lord Provost trailed in third place. One of the significant aspects of the result was that in this marginal situation, we had won support almost equally from both former Labour and former Tory voters.

The Labour Party had many full-time workers, including the candidate, canvassing and organising in the constituency for several weeks. The Tory Party made maximum use of the fact that their candidate was the Lord Provost, and he was given continuous supporting publicity in the Dundee papers. The Liberal Party put on the best show they could and produced a typical result, losing their deposit after confidently predicting that the contest was between them and Labour. The candidate for the Dundee Labour Party of Scotland was a drop-out from the SNP, an "empire-builder" from the 1968-70 period. He peddled his own brand of demands for Law and Order and for a Scottish Labour Government. It is galling, though unrealistic, to imagine that the D.L.P.S. vote of 1409 would have come to Gordon Wilson had they not contested. The same could be thought about the Liberal vote of 3653. I do not believe that the Liberal was given many nationalist or self-government votes, if any. It is conceivable that if the three candidates who lost their deposits (there was a colourful independent nationalist who polled 182 votes) had not stood, the Labour majority could have been greater. Of more importance in external factors was the sabotage of the TV discussion programmes on both the Independent TV networks and B.B.C. Both Tory and Labour refused to participate, so the planned programmes did not go ahead. The inference, which I believe to be justified, is that these two parties judged that their candidates were no match for the articulate, knowledgeable and confident Gordon Wilson. Another factor on which one can speculate is the possible result of earlier publication of the report by Parliament's Committee on Public Accounts on the totally inefficient handling of Scotland's oil wealth by both the Tory Government and its Labour predecessor. I have little doubt that it was deliberately held up until polling day (Thursday, 1st March) by the influence of Tory and Labour Parties. Because of its importance in relation to the Budget, I believe that it had to be published before Budget Day (Tuesday, 6th March).

The main topic of Gordon Wilson's campaign was the inescapable relationship between self-government and Scotland's North Sea oil wealth. The issues relating to the oil wealth are simple and they are clear. If Scotland had sovereignty similar to that of Norway, the oil in the Scottish sector of the North Sea and round the north and west coast of Scotland would belong by international law to the people of Scotland. Without self-government, the oil is 90% English under English control from London.

The English Parties (at least those members who realise the value of the oil) are delighted at this sudden access to untold wealth—not because they can use it to make up for generations of neglect and mis-government of Scotland, but because they can use it to rectify England's adverse trade balance, to pay their membership fees and strike bargains in the Common Market, and to help finance a tunnel under the English Channel, a better roadway system in and around London, a new London Airport and other similar mammoth projects with little or no benefit at all for the people of Scotland.

The way in which the Conservative Government has been virtually giving the oil rights away with hardly a squeak of complaint from the Labour Opposition is completely irresponsible. Other countries with oil resources control development in order to maintain a reasonably even flow of wealth over the longest possible period. One reason, of course, is to get England out of its economic mess as quickly as possible. In spite of this great wealth, we still have delegations from Scotland going to Germany and Japan and U.S.A. looking for clever men and wealthy banks to provide a few jobs for the poor unemployed of Scotland. What an insult to Scottish intelligence. What an insult to Scottish maturity. What a ridiculous situation for a wealthy industrialised country to be in. These emissaries would serve Scotland better by joining the SNP and working for self-government.

With its own Government right now, Scotland would certainly be rejoicing in its good fortune, but it certainly would not be allowing the indiscriminate and uncontrolled rape of Scotland's resources which is going on at the present time, nor would it be sending beggars abroad to creep and crawl for help. An independent Scotland would be doing as Norway is doing. It would control the oil development to ensure a reasonable flow of wealth to enhance the quality of life throughout the whole of Scotland, to provide work for the maximum number of Scots, to apply all the best principles of conservation and safeguards against pollution, and to prevent wherever possible the despoilation of the beauties of coast and countryside and town; and, above all, a Scottish Parliament would safeguard the indefinable qualities of Scottish community life, which are endangered by the threat of wholesale uncontrolled immigration from England and elsewhere.

Even at the lowest estimate, the wealth from the oil is fantastic. At the time of writing, our estimate of Government revenue from Scotland's oil in 1980 is £825 million. It could easily be four times that figure. This means that if you live in a community of about 13,000 people, your *annual* share in this extra £825 million will be around £2 million—and it will not be a loan with interest to pay and capital to repay. It amounts to at least as much as the total current expenditure by all the local authorities in Scotland, including what they get from Government. With the information which is available now, a Scottish Government would restrict any further exploration and developbent because the rate at which the wealth will be flowing out of the North Sea by 1980 would be more than enough for reasonable needs and surpluses.

The wealth of the oil destroys the myth that Scotland is too poor for self-government. It gives the Scots confidence to run their own affairs. It also makes my warning of ten years ago— "Time is not on our side"—a hundred times more apt because this oil wealth is attracting not only money and the power that wealth gives, from all over the world; it is also attracting people. It will allow the English Government to foster the migration of hundreds of thousands of people to Scotland and thus effectively overwhelm the Scottish nation. This is the most serious threat to Scotland today. England is about the most densely populated country in the world, with 900 people to the square mile; Scotland has 171. The lesson must surely be obvious. If you believe in the continuing existence of a Scottish nation, you must see that self-government now is imperative.

160

What is at stake is the existence, the *being* of a nation. That existence is a living, intangible force which is composed of many strands. A great number of these strands are being strained to breaking point. The essence of Scottish existence has its roots in the Celtic origins of the vast majority of the people of Scotland, whether we are talking of the warm community spirit of a mining village of the Lothians, of a tenement in Glasgow or of a scattered crofting township in the Hebrides. These are all strands of the life of the nation; but because of the anglicised universalism of the everyday culture of most of us who live in industrialised Scotland, it is in the Highlands and Islands that we find Scots with a living identity relating more clearly to our origins and history. How long will this remain as a living strand of our national being? At the present time, much of the Highlands is already alienated and the Government's plans to encourage the migration of hundreds of thousands of Englishmen to the North and North-East of Scotland will totally engulf and destroy the strands of Scottish community life.

I chose to open my Conference speech in Rothesay in 1972 with an attempt to speak Gaelic. The tongue is symbolic. I know very little Gaelic and I am certainly not in favour of making it compulsory throughout Scotland, but I want to learn Gaelic. I see that as a symbolic assertion of my being Scottish. Jean-Paul Sartre wrote of the Basques in Spain speaking their own language instead of Spanish: "It is a revolutionary act." In an article in the Basque magazine *Zutik* No. 61, translated by Harri Webb and published in the Welsh quarterly *Planet* No. 9, Sartre examines the position of the Basque people and their language and culture, argues strongly in favour of their political self-expression as a nation, and examines their responses to Spanish oppression.

The centralist Spaniard oppressors are Fascist and brutal. The Basque people are resolute and determined not to die as a nation. In comparison, the centralist English exploiters of the Scots are benevolent and patronising. They will willingly and even apologetically anglicise any Scot or Scotticism with a joke or smile; they will gladly appropriate our land and our resources such as oil, in completely sincere belief that they are doing us a favour; and the Scottish people are irresolute and polite, accustomed to being told by the clever, smiling English or by their representatives in Scotland that *they* know best what is good for Scotland. After all, *they* have managed Scotland's affairs for centuries. *They* are bound to be right.

161

In these examples, there is no comparison between the source of political power in the Basque language and that in Gaelic. But if the Scot by birth or by adoption recognises his peril he will acknowledge, if only in a word, that the roots of his community are *Scottish* and he will then draw on a new strength to assert the rights of *being* a citizen in the Scottish community.

Much of the trouble with Scotland stems from a feeling of inadequacy. We are Scots, and we know it and are not really ashamed of it, yet we do not assert it because we are so accustomed to the English negation of our being Scots, propagated morning, noon and night every day of the year. The media allow us a few hours or a few columns of Scottishness each week so long as it is not argument in favour of self-government, so long as such Scottishness is no more than an acceptable variant of Englishness, comparable with the variants of Yorkshire or Devon.

This environment is bound to make us Scots feel inadequate if we do not know clearly who we are and what our rights are. People contribute to society what is in them, in thought, in creativity, in action, in leadership; and what is in them is not only the sum of the aptitudes of heart and mind and matter with which they were endowed at birth—it includes the effect of the education (in its widest sense) they have received. If we are brought up to despise the environment of our childhood, to reject the language of our inheritance, to conform to some religious belief or other, to believe in the desirability of some political objective, we will have these things in us and will contribute to society accordingly. Unless we question some or all of these things, unless we try to be objective, unless we continue our education by seeking the forms of eternal value in our lives, we will remain in outlook more or less as our parents and as the teachers of our childhood left us.

My search for Truth is the quest of my life; and the principal setting of my quest is that fragment of the world called Scotland. I have examined and assessed the teachings of my childhood and of my later life, and from those which I have found good I have increased my sense of identity and my sense of belonging in the society in which I live. Some teachings I have rejected in my quest. Other teachings I have refurbished and polished and have found new strength in, like belief in the creativity and essential goodness of man; in the existence of a nation called Scotland, separate and distinct from all other nations, with all the rights and responsibilities of nationhood;

and in the desirability of organising society to establish unselfish equality with happy fulfilment and contentment as objectives, rather than seeking to promote only equality of opportunity which some people interpret as a licence for encouraging selfish competitive behaviour in which those who have an advantage are often encouraged to make use of it at the expense of others.

In political affairs, Scotland has several unique opportunities of great potential advantage in the 1970s, which she can benefit from without making use of them at the expense of others. Because Scotland without self-government is virtually part of England, the opportunities offer advantages to England as well and, as the English are in the dominating and controlling position over Scotland, they will be seizing the opportunities unless the Scots assert their rights strongly and uncompromisingly and say, "These are ours."

One of these great opportunities is the wealth of Scotland's oil. It is our oil. We can use it to our advantage, and to the advantage of the altruistic values we choose to enhance, at no one's expense but our own. A Scottish government's action to control the flow of oil at an annual level which would bring to Scotland in government revenues a handsome bonus equivalent to 15% of our country's national product would not be a selfish action. No other nation or group of nations would suffer from it. International means of control over such resources is certainly a desirable and unselfish objective, but in the 1970s we are nowhere near such an idealistic position and it is sound economic sense in international as well as national terms for all oil-exporting nations of the world to be prudent in the development and sale of what is a valuable non-renewable asset. That is what the other oil-producing countries are doing. That is what Scotland should be doing.

The industrial oil-consuming countries do not like this situation, so political pressure for real international control will undoubtedly build up, but we cannot deal with oil in isolation. Pressure for international control will spread to other things as well, and not only to forms of energy. We have seen recently Iceland's concern for conserving fish stocks and we have seen England's imperialistic gun-boat diplomacy in reaction. Fortunately, Scotland's interests are in line with those of Iceland and Norway. Here is another opportunity for Scotland in the 1970s —to participate in establishing much more effective control over the fishing grounds of the North-East Atlantic and North Sea.

163

International action will come, but only following the independent national initiative of the people of Iceland, who will be followed by the peoples of Norway and Denmark and, I hope, of Scotland.

So will it be in time with oil, but the present situation in relation to our oil resources is a *laissez-faire* free-for-all in which aggressive behaviour pays best in terms of financial gain for the oil companies, and in personal accumulation of capitalist wealth, irrespective of the damage which is done to the Scots. There is no sense in Scotland being altruistic in a kind of beggarly and sham holiness, generously letting England and the Common Market countries benefit from Scotland's oil at Scotland's expense, but that is exactly what is happening now, and will continue to happen so long as the Scots piously pin their political hopes on English parties and Westminster Government. The SNP's oil campaign posters are advertising the truth in capital letters—"WE SCOTS ARE THE MOST GENEROUS PEOPLE ON EARTH— WE ARE GIVING OUR OIL AWAY," and "SCOTLAND'S OIL—TO LONDON WITH LOVE?" Can anyone in Scotland really feel the love ironically referred to in that poster? Norway and Scotland are probably now the wealthiest nations in Europe, a position both countries could hold for many generations. Norway will receive 100% of the benefit of Norway's oil. The way the Norwegians are going about it, they will be exporting oil for decades after Scotland's oil is all used up, if the Scots allow the English to take all the advantages of Scotland's oil at the breakneck speed of development and exploitation the latter desire.

Let us return to a question of basic belief—are we Scots or is our nationality a second-class English form called British? To be effective as human beings, to have a sense of fulfilment in society, to have a sense of belonging, a sense of identity, we must *be* ourselves fully to be whole men and women. The oil poses the fundamental question more emphatically than almost any other factor of recent times. It is a question of "Who are we?" If we are Scots, then Scotland's oil will be ours by asserting our right, our democratic honourable moral right to choose to have our own Parliament and Government to control that oil and to make the best use possible of the opportunities it brings to us. If we are to be "British," then we should be happy to let London continue to exploit that part of the United Kingdom called Scotland which it has so unashamedly and profitably exploited for the past 250 years; and we should be equally happy to see the national community of Scotland disappear.

What other opportunity do the people of Scotland have in the 1970s? The opportunity of being "in Europe," as the pro-Marketeers say, is a two-sided one also, like the oil, and the assessment of it is very similar. As in the case of the oil, this matter poses the basic question, "Are we Scots or are we English?" By choosing to be Scots we must choose again to rule our own destiny through a Scottish Parliament; thus we will have a voice of our own in the affairs of Europe, and the right and the power to defend our interests and to participate in all negotiations affecting them.

I am not happy about the concept of the European Economic Community as it was founded on fear, on authoritarianism and on greed. It has been dressed up in fanfares and terms of inter-nationalism but the words "Brotherhood of Man" have rarely if ever been used in relation to the Common Market. That would have been too much of an untruth to stomach. It is a power-bloc monolithic system and I would not want to join such an organisation in the hope of changing it from the inside, even if there were real grounds for hope that change could be effected. Such change would require real power bases, but the financial interlocking of Western Germany, France, England and Italy, supported by the U.S.A., makes the establishment of other economic or political power bases very difficult to imagine in the foreseeable future, without the force of democracy, which is not yet effective in the institutions of the E.E.C.

There is some hope in the unrest in the Netherlands, where criticism of the bureaucratic and undemocratic control of the E.E.C. has long been voiced. There is hope that other such voices will be raised in the E.E.C. and, with participation in the Common Market institutions which self-government would give to Scotland, our voice would no doubt be heard along with the others who sought democratic effectiveness. All these voices together might actuate change in Europe but they will require power-backing which, in E.E.C. terms, means financial and economic strength. An independent Scotland, with its oil wealth, with its industrial strength, with its freedom to be itself again, will be in a position of strength. We will not require hand-outs from anyone. We have never had any before, from England or from any other nation, and it is totally unrealistic to think that the E.E.C. might subsidise Scotland. Not only is it unrealistic, it is demeaning to think thus, for we certainly do not need sub-sidies. There are many other countries who *deserve* help. Scotland should be giving, not receiving.

The opportunities before Scotland in the 1970s are all linked together. They all depend on the will of the people of Scotland to be a nation again. Not just a provincial part of the "one nation" of the English political parties, but to be a nation again, dynamically, fully, clear of the negation and alienation which have for so long tried to persuade the Scots that to be British is to be internationlist. In fact, it is to be English.

When our children are taught English History instead of Scottish History; when almost every effort of education, from the infant classes to the universities, seems bent on promoting the "one nation" theory and habitual practice of the English Tory and Labour Parties, is it any wonder that people who believe in Scotland feel alienated?

When we see the influence of most of the daily newspapers and television and radio programmes as English, in reporting news, in dealing with current affairs, in entertainment of all kinds; when we see Scottish dole queues that are always twice as long as English dole queues; when we see people forced to emigrate, knowing that Scotland's population has risen only 2½% in 20 years while England's has risen 11%, Norway's has risen 18% and the U.S.A.'s has risen 33% in the same period; when we know that in spite of Scotland having had the resources of wealth and the skills, the educational institutions and the brains to have averted that unemployment and that emigration; when we perceive that the decline and stagnation have persisted, all because of the "one nation" theory and practice of the English Parties, is it any wonder that people who believe in Scotland feel alienated?

When we see the deep water facilities of the Clyde ignored; when we comprehend the threat of mass destruction inherent in the seven nuclear bases sited in Scotland, without the consent of the people of Scotland; when we see Scotland as a tourist attraction promoted abroad as *Angleterre*; when we see factory after factory close down after English take-overs; when we see industry after industry hacked about to fit into an English Plan; when we see Budget Day after Budget Day in Westminster prescribing medicine for the English sickness of inflation when Scotland needs the opposite encouragement, having quite different conditions including no balance of payments problem; when we see the possibility of Scotland's great oil wealth not benefiting our country, our people, our nation, and all because of the "one nation" theory and practice of the English Parties, is it any wonder that people who believe in Scotland feel alienated?

In his inaugural address as Rector of Glasgow University, James Reid defined the effects of what he meant by alienation. "It is the cry of men who feel themselves the victims of blind, economic forces beyond their control. It is the frustration of ordinary people excluded from the processes of decision-making." I would add alien political and cultural forces to the economic forces, with the proviso that I do not believe that the alien political forces are blind.

For over ten years, I have taken part in the struggle against English political forces in Scotland which would alienate me and my children from our own heritage and prevent us from freely exercising our rights to be Scottish in the ways in which the people of other nations express their rights. With the rights go responsibilities, I know, but I am not afraid of the responsibilities. Neither are hundreds of thousands of other Scots like me. In my eleven years' stent, I have seen Scotland's national party grow and develop. It has not just become larger, it has been like the steel under the hammer.

As steel is heated, then forged, then heated again and hammered again in a repetitive process, it is refined and shaped and hardened for exacting and testing work. So it is with the Scottish National Party, heated in the total cultural heritage of Scotland, both historic and current. It is shaped between the anvil of knowledge and the hammer of determination. Its effectiveness is tested in use by experience. Each time it goes back to the furnace, the knowledge is improved, the determination is strengthened.

Throughout the work, the fire is kept burning by the will of a nation to live. That fire must never be extinguished, suffocated by the alien forces who smile benevolently as they take over. On the outcome of all our effort depends the survival of a nation.